EDGAR HARRISON

SOLDIER - PATRIOT AND
ULTRA WIRELESS OPERATOR TO
WINSTON CHURCHIL

Edgar Harrison – Soldier, Patriot and Ultra Wireless Operator to Winston Churchill ©
Copyright 2008 by Geoffrey Pidgeon

A catalogue record of this book is available from the British Library

Paperback Edition: September 2008

ISBN: 978-0-9560515-0-9

To order additional copies of this book please visit: http://www.geoffreypidgeon.com

Published by: Arundel Books
3 Arundel House, Courtlands, Sheen Road, Richmond. TW10 5AS
Email: info@geoffreypidgeon.com
http://www.geoffreypidgeon.com

Designed by: Prestige Press
Web: http://www.prestige-press.com

EDGAR HARRISON

SOLDIER - PATRIOT AND
ULTRA WIRELESS OPERATOR TO
WINSTON CHURCHILL

Geoffrey Pidgeon

Author of 'The Secret Wireless War'
A wartime member of MI6 (Section VIII), SCU1, SCU11/12 and DWS.

Arundel Books

DEDICATION

This book is dedicated to Edgar's widow, Florence Harrison, who asked me to follow Edgar's request to turn his drafts and notes into a book and publish it. She has moreover, since been a tower of strength to me with her continued support and particularly with research.

Edgar Harrison of MI6 (Section VIII),
shown during World War II as an officer in the Royal Corps of Signals.

The pictures on the front cover are: Sir Winston Churchill, Edgar Harrison (circa 1939) and 'Jimmy' the Badge of the Royal Corps of Signals. The picture on the back cover is of Edgar – age 89 – at Kalamata before delivering the Oration to the annual memorial ceremony – held at the site of the last stand by the Allies in mainland Greece – Kalamata 1941. The stripes are in the colours of Edgar's beloved Royal Corps of Signals and represent land, sea and air.

Geoffrey Pidgeon, Richmond, Surrey. September 2008

CONTENTS

Appendices:
I have tried, so far as possible, to ensure the chapters follow the story as told by Edgar in his draft work sent to me. There were many gaps, as I explained in the Prologue but these have been filled – so far as I can – by research. I appreciate some explanations were necessary but I set out to avoid adding undue text not directly associated with Edgar, within the chapters. However, I felt that in some cases more fulsome explanations were necessary and Appendix 1 and 2 are good examples.

Acknowledgements

I am deeply grateful to a number of people and organisations for their assistance in producing this book. Their help came in many forms including research, information, introductions and images. I hope I have included all their names here but ask forgiveness if anyone has been omitted.

Florence Harrison: First and foremost, I wish to record my thanks to Florence Harrison who, having asked me to continue to write Edgar's story, has taken up all my challenges in finding obscure details for me. She has researched books referring to a specific problem in her local library and helped in a whole multitude of ways. Not least, has been her careful editing of the drafts I presented to her as well as the corrections and suggestions that arose from her work.

Jane Pidgeon: Secondly, my deep appreciation must go to my wife – of sixty years – Jane! She has been patient whilst I 'disappeared' yet again into my study to work on this book. Jane even put up for three years with my taking my laptop on our holidays abroad, so I could make progress with it. She has read, edited and commented on all the work as it went along.

Yvonne Willway: Before he died, Edgar asked that I record his thanks to their friend Yvonne Willway who had so kindly typed up his notes for him. I would add my own grateful thanks.

Caroline Wakefield: Caroline took the draft notes I received and typed them into digital form so that I could more easily work on them. At the same time, she undertook the (tricky) task of turning the notes from first person into the third person.

Winnie Graham: Widow of John Graham (another of the 'F' Company boys from 1929) for her gracious permission to use the two photographs of the wireless room at Peking.

Sir Patrick Leigh Fermor for his introduction to Antony Beevor.

Antony Beevor: Antony is a well known author of many books including best-sellers such as Stalingrad; Berlin: The Downfall 1945; The Battle for Spain (The Spanish Civil War); Crete: The Battle and the Resistance. After completing Army training at Sandhurst, Antony became a serving officer in the 11th Hussars. Edgar went to Tidworth in the 1930s as a wireless operator in 'F' Troop Cavalry Division Signals who were attached to the 11th Hussars PAO (Prince Albert's Own). Antony helped me make contact with their Museum at Tidworth. He also allowed me to quote from his book on Crete. I am very deeply in his debt.

Stephen Courtney: Curator of Photographs at the Royal Naval Museum, HM Naval Base at Portsmouth for his kindness in locating and providing pictures for me. In particular I was delighted to have pictures of HMS Kandahar that picked Edgar up in the Mediterranean, and the submarine HMS Perseus that collected him from Yugoslavia.

Christina Pouliadis and Katerina Orfanidi of Grande Bretange Hotel in Athens for sending me the splendid book showing the history of this famous hotel, and for their helpful research into the source of photographs. They also put me in touch with Petros Gaitanos.

Petros Gaitanos for his kind permission to use the photograph taken from the roof of the Grande Bretagne Hotel in Athens in its splendid anniversary book. This picture is remarkable being just how Edgar would have seen it – with the Acropolis in the distance.

Kostas Kontothanasis who found pictures for me of the type of railway engine used on the Port Argos to Kalamata line, and of Kalamata railway station.

Nikos Zervis for the drawing of German guns in action against Allied troops near the harbour at Kalamata during the battle for the port.

New Zealand Land and Survey Department for allowing me to use the plan of Kalamata harbour during the last hours of the Allied retreat from mainland Greece.

Larry Crozier for the picture showing the interior of the period railway signal box.

Dennis Machin – a fellow member with Edgar in 'F' Company at Catterick – in 1929: for photographs of its barrack room and other pictures.

Ann Butler for her pictures of Mihailovic, the Chetniks and other pictures of wartime Yugoslavia.

Sandra Marsh of the Churchill Archives at Churchill College in Cambridge for the two fine pictures of Winston Churchill taken with troops in the North African desert.

Nicoletta Daoulis: Whilst we were on holiday last year at the Athena Royal Beach Hotel in Cyprus, Nicoletta helped me by contacting people in Greece for me – in Greek!

Ian Procter of the Photographic Archives Section of The Imperial War Museum in London for his patience and various introductions, including to the Royal Naval Museum at Portsmouth.

Colonel (Retd.) Cliff Walters of the Royal Corps of Signals: When I agreed to write this book I contacted Colonel Walters. He was then in charge of the Royal Signals

Museum at Blandford Camp, Blandford Forum in Dorset, and he was able to give me most helpful information.

Anthony Gambier-Parry for the splendid photograph of his grandfather – Major-General Michael Gambier-Parry. Anthony had earlier found a picture of our 'boss' Brigadier Richard Gambier-Parry (Michael's brother) in uniform and I used it in the second and subsequent prints of 'The Secret Wireless War' – as well as in this book about Edgar Harrison.

David Fletcher and Janice Tait of The Tank Museum at Bovingdon for first finding and then giving their kind permission for the use of the pictures in Chapter 14 to illustrate Edgar's work with tanks in the Ukraine – whilst on the 'Way Mission' to the Soviet Union.

Jack Valenti: He is the chief historian, coordinator of equipment and show organizer of the Long Range Desert Group Preservation Society in California. He has helped in numerous ways including contacts for pictures and background information of this remarkable unit that fought so bravely – initially in the Sahara Desert. Its base was the Kufra Oasis deep in the desert – some 400 miles south from the North African coast. The LRDG Society published an excellent article by courtesy of **Trevor Constable** and I sought permission to use parts of it but neither Jack Valenti or myself could trace him. Should that happen later then I shall gladly publish his name in a future edition.

Tobias Gibson: He supplied the excellent drawing of a LRDG vehicle for me, as well as valuable information about LRDG. I am very grateful to have this detailed illustration.

Yannis Samatas of Explore Crete who has been so helpful with pictures from his archive of the fighting between the German paratroops and the Allies defending Crete in 1941.

Aneeta Pidgeon: Our daughter-in-law Aneeta is an interior designer but was persuaded to make the special maps required for the book. They are right for the purpose and are intended to show just Edgar's travels so therefore do not include many other towns or cities.

Lt. Col. (Retd.) Michael Butler MBE – Royal Corps of Signals. Mike has been of great help especially over detailed matters about the Royal Signals and has been a mine of information. In 1945 he enlisted into the Boy's Squadron of the Corps at the age of 14 – the same as Edgar. He saw service as a a technician and served as Foreman of Signals in Cyprus and Germany. He attained the rank of Warrant Officer Class 1 and in 1970 was commissioned as a Technical Officer reaching the rank of Lieutenant Colonel. He continued to serve as a Retired Officer in Germany until final retirement age 65 in 1996. Mike works as a volunteer at the Royal Corps of Signals at Blandford.

Major (Retd.) Robin Boon of the King's Royal Hussars: He is Regimental Secretary and based at *HorsePower*, the Museum of The King's Royal Hussars in Winchester. Edgar was attached to the 11th Hussars in the 1930s but after World War II, various regimental amalgamations found them eventually incorporated in the King's Royal Hussars.

Ian Chatfield, Curator of the Queen's Royal Surrey Regiment Museum at Clandon Park, Guildford; for the picture of the British Legation in Peking in the 1930s. The wireless room used by Edgar was inside this building.

Brenda Pratten; who provided information of Yugoslavia and the LRDG.

Pat Hawker is a wartime colleague from MI6 (Section VIII): He was undoubtedly a great support to me with my first book 'The Secret Wireless War' and his knowledge of the agents' wireless sets we made at Whaddon Hall has been of considerable assistance here as well.

Pauline and Richard Winward: They are the owners of Whaddon Hall today and their support for my earlier book 'The Secret Wireless War' has been useful in writing this book as well.

Western Mail and Echo for kind permission to use the photograph of Windsor Colliery.

Mavis Batey is one of the original members of the Bletchley Park codebreakers having worked for Dilwynn Knox as a cryptographer and she specialised in the Abwehr Spy Enigma. She was also involved with his team in Italian cyphers and is justly proud that their work resulted in the Naval victory over the Italians at the Battle of Matapan. Mavis continues to advise Bletchley Park on its wartime history and has been of immense help to me - on this on on many other aspects of the work of BP and Whaddon Hall.

Simon Greenish is the CEO of the Bletchley Park Trust and is largely responsible for the improving fortunes of Bletchley Park. I am grateful to him for permission to launch this book in Bletchley Park Mansion and for his general support.

Wilf Neal: He was attached to General Patton's 3rd US Army and has continued to assist in my research into the operational side of SCU/SLUs. This is also the case with **Len Digby** who was a wireless operator in the SCU/SLU with General Simpson's 9th US Army. I am grateful to both these wartime colleagues.

David Pearman. Last, but by no means least, I want to thank my friend David who has been so helpful from the outset of this project. He is the proprietor of Prestige Press who are specialist publishers and book designers. His knowledge and understanding of the publishing world have been of immense benefit.

I have made every effort to acknowledge correct copyright and/or origin of material and images where applicable. Some information came via friends and it has proved impossible to establish the original source or author. Any errors or omissions are unintentional and should be reported to me and I will arrange for corrections to appear in any reprint.

Glossary

Abwehr. (Literally 'defence'). This was Admiral Canaris's military intelligence organisation similar to our MI6.

ATS. Auxiliary Territorial Service. The women's service in the Army.

BEF. The British Expeditionary Force, the Army units sent to France soon after the outbreak of war in 1939 and withdrawn from the Continent in 1940.

Boniface. A fictitious name given to deciphered Enigma traffic early on, implying that the information was being received from an agent named Boniface. The intelligence was referred to as coming from 'Source Boniface' thus ensuring that nobody suspected we were actually breaking Enigma itself. Many military Commanders were fed in intelligence coming from 'a well placed agent' and frequently the name 'Boniface' used. However, only the highest level of intelligence was later designated 'Ultra'.

Boss. You may be intrigued to see the word 'Boss' used. I do not recall hearing anyone refer to a person above one – as being one's 'superior officer' although with differing ranks, that was technically the case. Perhaps that is because I was not connected to the military side at Little Horwood.

However, in SCU circles Richard Gambier-Parry was 'The Boss'. To the more senior members he was often referred to as 'Pop' but not directly to him. See below.

'C' is the Head of SIS (or MI6). Also sometimes shown as 'CSS'.

CPO is capable of two interpretations:

The first use of the initials CPO is Chief Petty Officer, a senior non-commissioned officer in the Royal Navy. In the book, it will refer to those who joined Section VIII from the Navy's wireless units.

Secondly, the initials CPO can also refer to Chief Passport Officer. This was the title of the head of the Passport Office before the war as a cover for SIS attached to Embassies in major cities across the world.

'CSS'. Chief of SIS (or MI6).

DMI. Director of Military Intelligence.

DWS. Diplomatic Wireless Service. This was created out of Section VIII by Gambier-Parry at the end of the war and 'sold' as a complete communication system to the Foreign Office to handle both diplomatic and covert traffic.

DX-er. An amateur wireless operator who was used to working with weak Morse signals over long distances.

Enigma. This was a commercially available cypher machine used by the German services: Army, Navy and Air Force, as well as the Abwehr, Police and Gestapo. They were totally convinced – right throughout the war – that others could not read messages sent by this process.

GC&CS. Government Code & Cypher School. It was a descendant of Room 40 of the Admiralty that did such sterling work on codes in World War I. This pre-war code-breaking organisation, was first based in Queen's Gate in London, but in the thirties moved into 54, Broadway, the Headquarters of SIS.

Gees. The almost universally applied name for the base at Little Horwood, part of which was housed in the premises built by Mr. Gee of Gee Walker Slater, a prominent building contractor in prewar London.

G-P. A commonly used shorthand description for Brigadier Richard Gambier-Parry, Head of MI6 Section VIII throughout the war. However, I will not be using it in the chapters that follow.

Head of Station. The is the title given to the chief SIS officer, usually at an Embassy. Before the war he was more often referred to as the CPO or Chief Passport Officer.

HRO. A high grade American wireless receiver made by the National Company which had a distinctive removable coil bank change. Used by Section VIII in great numbers, by interceptors around the country, and by our stations abroad.

Hudson. The Lockheed Hudson was supplied to the RAF for a variety of duties, including Coastal Command. It was used by squadrons based at Tempsford in Cambridgeshire to carry SOE & SIS agents into and out of Europe.

The SIS used them to work to its agents on the ground through the Whaddon-designed wireless equipment called 'Ascension' its air-to-ground wireless system. Edgar apparently flew in one to and from Kufra.

ISLD. Inter Services Liaison Department. The cover name for the SIS presence in active military zones like the Mediterranean, North Africa, the Middle East and India/Burma.

Main Line Station or Main Line Traffic. This name appears a number of times and refers to a wireless station and the traffic it handled. In Richard Gambier-Parry's reorganisation just before World War II, he ensured that the wireless station at an Embassy could handle both diplomatic and covert messages. During the war the name continued to be used although the station might well not be at an Embassy. 'Hut 1' at Bletchley Park handled Main Line Traffic before it was moved to the newly built station in the fields in front of Whaddon Hall.

After the war, an Embassy wireless station divided its traffic into 'Prodrome' – Foreign Office or into 'Medal' that was MI6 traffic.

MI5. The security branch of Britain's Intelligence Services. Mostly concerned with home affairs.

MI6. This is the external branch of Britain's Secret Intelligence Services. The public and media use the term MI6 but within the service it calls itself 'The Firm' or SIS.

MkI / MkIII / MkV / MkVII / MkIX and MkX. Numbers of various agent's sets produced by Section VIII at its Whaddon or Little Horwood workshops. In the case of the MkI it was first produced at Barnes and then later at Funny Neuk.

Morse. Signalling by code in which each letter is formed by a combination of dots and dashes. The best-known letters in Morse are SOS (...——...). It was normally sent by wireless telegraphy but Edgar used a torch with which to signal ships at Kalamata. (Greece)

NCO. Non commissioned officer. Any rank between a Lance-Corporal and a Regimental Sergeant-Major.

One-time pads. A method of encoding messages that made them virtually indecypherable by the enemy as they required both sender and receiver to have an identical pad of tear off sheets. The sender indicates the relevant sheet to the receiver and the sheets were destroyed after use.

The one-time pad was probably the safest of all cypher systems from the point of view of security - although slow and cumbersome in use. Later on, SLUs used the RAF designed Typex machine which was somewhat similar to the Enigma. It was faster to use than a one-time pad and very safe.

Passport Office. Cover name for SIS units abroad, usually attached to an Embassy.

PCO. Passport Control Officer. A member of the staff at the Passport Office but employed by SIS.

Pop. Perhaps surprisingly, this is the way we usually referred to Brigadier Richard Gambier-Parry amongst ourselves, although not to his face, and absolutely not by the more junior staff there - like me! It arose from his own constant use of the name in such things as his Christmas message to us and in personal letters to his more senior staff. Also see 'Boss'.

Rockex. A cypher machine manufactured under utmost secrecy at Hanslope Park (SCU3). Phased out in the early 1980s.

SCU. Special Communication Unit. The later pseudo-military name for Section VIII's wartime communications to disguise both its origin and its tasks. It is important to remember, that although SSUs (now SCUs), were created to be the conduit for Ultra traffic, Section VIII already had numerous other tasks to perform in the communication field. However, these were then conducted mostly under the umbrella name of Special Communication Units.

Section VIII was the communication department (or 8th Section), of MI6 during the war years. From time to time, I will say MI6 (Section VIII), and sometimes just Section VIII.

SIGINT. Signals intelligence. The highest-grade of SIGINT later became known as Ultra.

Sigm. A Signalman. The Royal Corps of Signals equivalent of a private soldier.

SIS. Secret Intelligence Service but more commonly referred to as MI6. When abroad we were referred to as members of ISLD (Inter Service Liaison Department).

SLU. Special Liaison Unit. The name given by Fred. W. Winterbotham, to the units handling Ultra traffic. These were often mobile and would then be coupled with an SCU wireless unit. But, there were a number of fixed ones in the UK, as in the St. James Park underground complex, and at RAF Fighter Command.

Some fixed SLUs received their information directly from Bletchley Park by teleprinter but sometimes had a support team from SCU as a wireless backup and the 'Dugout' in St. James Park in Westminster is a good example where this existed.

'Special Liaison Unit' or SLU later became the name for the unit handling Ultra that would contain a wireless facility (usually but not always staffed by the Army), controlled by Section VIII, and a cypher facility supplied by Winterbotham from RAF cypher training schools. Quite frequently, the mobile units were now being described as SCU/SLU.

In the Mediterranean area of operations there would have been a greater mix of the three services but the control always remained the same: the wireless side by Gambier-Parry's Section VIII, and the cypher via Winterbotham's own connection with MI6 - Section

IV (Air). SLUs existed in Brisbane, Delhi, Calcutta, Cairo and other centres. Some had teleprinter connections direct to Bletchley Park and others relied on wireless.

SOE. Several departments of the Foreign Office and the War Office were merged in July 1940 to form an organisation to counter the Nazis by subversion. This became known as Special Operations Executive or SOE for short. The very existence of this unit was one of the best-kept secrets of the war. Its headquarters was set up at 64 Baker Street, London W1.

SOE's purpose was to train agents to be sent into France, and other occupied countries, to link with local resistance units and to cause sabotage. There was therefore, a fundamental difference between SIS agents, who were trained to quietly collect intelligence and pass it back to London, and SOE agents who were largely intent on creating havoc. There was a long-standing and tangible friction between the two organisations.

Their agents were issued with special suitcase wireless transmitters and receivers that looked like a normal piece of luggage. Initially, Section VIII at Whaddon provided these but later they produced their own sets.

SOG. Special Operations Group. A division of SCU1 especially responsible for handling traffic to commands in the field. Its main transmitter was Windy Ridge.

SSU. Special Signals Unit. The first name given to the militarised Section VIII in 1940 but it was changed in 1941, to SCU - Special Communications Unit. It was thought the initials SSU might be regarded as standing for Secret Service Unit.

There were also unpleasant connotations, with the German use of SS. In 1940 the letters SSU appeared painted - as the unit's Army designation - over a blue and white badge on the wing of its military vehicles. These were later removed and replaced with the initials SCU.

Station X. The code for Barnes wireless station before the war. Later used for a few months as the name of the SIS station at Bletchley Park, before it was transferred to Whaddon Hall, in late 1939.

Traffic. Throughout the book you will see reference to 'traffic' and this is the name given to the messages or 'traffic' in Morse or plain language being handled between wireless operators.

Typex. Cypher machine in use at Bletchley Park and in SLUs, along with one time pads.

Ultra. Is the name given to the messages gathered by our various Y services from the German use of Enigma cypher machines, and the intelligence then emanating from the codebreakers at Bletchley Park.

Depending upon importance, their output was marked 'Secret' / 'Most Secret' / 'Top Secret' then later 'Ultra Secret' – as being the most secret of all. It is from the latter that the name 'Ultra' was derived. This name appeared only later in the war but I have used it through most of the book since we all know what is meant by the word. It is succinct and understood by everyone today as a generic term but bear in mind it was most certainly not in universal use at the time.

Wherever possible, the handling of Ultra traffic was kept separate from the 'Main Line' station at Whaddon Hall, on the grounds of security. Certainly, all Ultra traffic for commanders in the field went out via the 'Windy Ridge' wireless station near the Church in Whaddon Village. However, there were occasions when the two became mixed up, such as in Greece towards the end, and in the Crete battles that followed.

WAAF. Women's Auxiliary Air Force. Many hundreds were employed in numerous roles, including teleprinter operators, in the 'Y' Service, and so on.

Winterbotham. Wing Commander Frederick Winterbotham, Head of MI6 (Section IV) Air, who was charged by 'C' (Stewart Menzies) to ensure the total security of Ultra traffic.

Wrens. Women's Royal Naval Service. They carried out many tasks on interception and at Bletchley Park on the Bombes and Colossus.

XW. 'XW' was the call sign for Whaddon used by all stations from around the world, after MI6 had taken over Whaddon Hall in November 1939. It had previously been 'X' – the MI6 name for the wireless station it had built in the tower of Bletchley Park Mansion in 1938/9. The transfer of that station to Whaddon Hall was completed by March 1940.

However, I suggest 'X' refers to the Main Line station in the grounds of the Hall, with the 'W' standing for Whaddon. All traffic intended for MI6 in London used 'XW' as the call sign. Edgar Harrison recalls in 'The Secret Wireless War' – that this was used for all his traffic intended for London including that involving Mr. Churchill. Others, including Bill Miller who, during the war, was the covert ISLD wireless operator in Tangier, also confirm this in the same book – see Chapter 28 – entitled 'Tea with the Germans'.

Y Service. This is the Wireless Intercept service that collected the raw wireless messages transmitted by the German forces, where the traffic was being encyphered by Enigma machines. The initial 'Y' comes from the two words Wireless Interception - wi or 'Y'.

The first requirement of the 'Codebreakers' was the interception and recording of the myriad messages arising from the thousands of Enigma machines with their associated wireless sets – across the whole German military machine.

The organisations supplying this service were spread right across the country. The majority of the operators listening in and recording the German traffic were members of the women's services ATS, Wrens and WAAF. They were controlled by the Army, the Navy and the RAF but came under the umbrella of a 'WT Board'. This included representatives of the intelligence sections from each of the forces and from MI6 and MI5. The intercepted messages were then sent in thousands daily – by teleprinter or despatch rider to Bletchley Park – depending on the priority given.

In addition, there were messages emanating from Germany's most secret organisations the Secret Police/Gestapo and the Abwehr – broadly speaking – their equivalents of our MI5 and MI6. These were gathered by the Radio Security Service (RSS). To begin with, the RSS was part of MI5 then absorbed into MI6 (Section VIII) and finally became known as SCU3. Latterly it was based mostly at Hanslope in North Bucks, not far from Bletchley Park, and at Arkley near Barnet. The Head of SCU3 (and RSS) was Lt. Col. 'Ted' Maltby of Section VIII who was also Deputy to Brigadier Richard Gambier-Parry.

The memorial to fallen Allied troops at Kalamata, Greece

Edgar Harrison 1915-2005
Giving the Oration in memory of Allied troops who fell at the battle of Kalamata in Greece 1942

Amongst Edgar's many wartime adventures, he was nearly captured by the Germans at Kalamata where the last battle on mainland Greece was fought by the Allied and Greek forces.

Edgar went back to Kalamata each year where he gave the Oration at the annual ceremony to the fallen Allied British, Australian, New Zealand, Cypriot and Greek troops in the Battle of Kalamata 1941.

The above photograph of Edgar was taken during the Oration, in his 90th year.

PROLOGUE

Whilst I speak of Edgar as a wartime colleague, in fact, although we had corresponded for a few years, I did not meet him until early 2001. However, I already knew something about him, having worked closely with his brother Wallace at Whaddon Hall in the MI6 (Section VIII) Mobile Construction unit in 1944.

From 1998 to 2000, David White (curator of the Bletchley Park Wireless Museum) and I lobbied the Bletchley Park Trust to allow me to place a portrait of Brigadier Sir Richard Gambier-Parry KCMG, Head of MI6 (Section VIII), in the hallway of the Mansion there.

In late 2000, Bletchley Park Trust kindly agreed that a portrait and the accompanying eulogy I had written would be accepted. Therefore, I sent out invitations to as many of our old colleagues as we could trace. I had already found a few and these were helping me in the research of my proposed book to be called – 'The Secret Wireless War'.

The presentation was to take place in January 2001 and Edgar was high on my list. I was delighted when, in spite of ill health, he accepted and attended with his wife Florence. There, in front of many of our old colleagues, I invited him to assist me in unveiling the portrait. Afterwards he spoke in most moving terms about Richard Gambier-Parry – our boss – known as 'Pop' and of the deep affection we had all felt towards him. Both portrait and the eulogy were subsequently placed in the hallway of the Mansion.

My aim in presenting his portrait to Bletchley Park was to record the part his unit played in the interception of German wireless traffic – particularly that of the Abwehr – and its role in disseminating Bletchley Park's output as 'Ultra' traffic – to our military Commanders in the field. I believe strongly that the success of Bletchley Park and its 'Codebreakers' was actually trilateral.

It was formed by the various 'Y' units that intercepted German Army, Navy and Luftwaffe wireless traffic, the brilliant work done by the 'Codebreakers' at Bletchley Park and the work of MI6 (Section VIII) – charged with its dissemination out to our military Commanders in the field.

When my book was ready for its launch at Bletchley Park in September 2003, I again invited Edgar and other colleagues, particularly those who had contributed to the book. It was a remarkable turnout and during the launch I presented him with a copy. He then spoke for about twenty minutes about his long military career – to the audience packed into the ballroom of the Bletchley Park Mansion. Those who were present still use the same expression to describe the experience – 'You could hear a pin drop!'

He had earlier written the story of his life for his family and entitled it 'The First 60 Years' and had five copies made but being his full life story, it naturally did not concentrate on his wartime career. He also contributed a chapter to my book 'The Secret Wireless War'. But, in 2005 when he was already 90, I finally prevailed upon him to record those wartime memories he so briefly described at my book launch.

By June 2005, he had dictated a number of events from his life in rough chapter form that he then asked me to edit, form into a book and have printed. At that time, he wanted only some copies made for himself – plus a few to be made available for colleagues – if I thought they might be of interest!

I undertook to edit and publish it for him but even a preliminary glance at his drafts, showed that it was too interesting and historically important to restrict publication in that way.

He accepted my view and agreed I should have it published for a wider audience. So, over a period, we exchanged comments on the first one or two chapters. Sadly he died in November 2005 – leaving the vast majority of the notes untouched. I later discussed this with his widow Florence and she asked me to finish turning it into book – a task that I readily accepted.

I had pointed out to Edgar that his drafts left much of his story incomplete and those were the main points raised in our exchanges. For example, later on I found in his draft about Greece – a brief mention to the effect he was rescued at sea and put ashore on Crete. In that same draft, he mentions the German airborne landings on Crete, orders given later to destroy his equipment and take ship to Alexandria. All this he dealt with in just a few lines.

Nowhere, does he mention the vital work being done by him and his colleagues before the actual invasion. Nor did he record those few days on the island – under the most frightening and dangerous attack – or of its part in the history of Ultra.

We found similar 'gaps' in other stories and often these are about the intense warfare in which he became involved. He was wounded during the fighting in Greece, we know for example he was in fierce fighting in Yugoslavia with colleagues killed and wounded alongside him but that was not very detailed in his notes. We must remember he was a signals expert and not primarily trained or expected to become mixed up in close order combat – but he most certainly was!

I have tried to fill some of the gaps with help from his earlier notes, some from research material and from other colleagues. As a result, the book has been written – in the only way that seems feasible to me – as a biography. I added considerable detail into a number of the chapters where I thought it completed his outlined story. It is an advantage that I worked at Whaddon Hall and knew most of those he refers to from there, such as Bob Hornby, 'Spuggy' Newton, Charles Emary and so on. Nevertheless, although now very considerably enlarged, the book itself is still closely based on Edgar's story. Though so much detail has been added, I feel I should not consider myself the author but more perhaps just an Editor!

In the chapter on Greece, he relates his interview with our boss Richard Gambier-Parry on being sent to contact his brother Major-General Michael Gambier-Parry in Greece. He was told 'For this, I could have sent any one of your colleagues, but I considered that you are the best for this particular task'. Firstly, he was a first class wireless operator but just as importantly at the time, he was one of the very few of Gambier-Parry's staff with any military training. It had no doubt been one of the reasons why he was earlier instructed to escort the agent to Norway and then to support the wireless room at the Brussels Embassy – just before the German Blitzkrieg.

During his short address at my book launch, Edgar joked about the number of times he had been forced to retreat during his service with Section VIII and said he felt like writing a book entitled 'Beating the retreats!' That then, is the sub-title of this book and again it reflects on his good humour and great courage.

I think it is important to remember that when I finally persuaded Edgar to dictate the full story of his military career he was then 90 and he was relating events going back many years. However, with the continued help from Florence with research and comment, I have done everything possible to ensure accuracy – so far as I can – sadly without the real author!

To avoid breaking up the flow of the story, I decided to use a number of appendices to explain many subjects in more detail. My aim is to add information for those interested in understanding the background to these major and important matters. I do not pretend for a moment that they are the definitive story, some may say 'simplistic' but they may help explain some of the action.

In one or two cases – such as the dreadful civil war in Yugoslavia – you will find many books whose authors back the Tito version of events whilst others support Mihailovic or even the Ustasi of Croatia. Whatever view you take, one thing becomes very clear. Besides fighting the German and Italian occupying army – tens of thousands of innocent people were slaughtered by these factions – because of their ethnic group, politics, religion – or sometimes simply because they were living in the wrong place.

Because Edgar found the civil war in Yugoslavia so perplexing I have devoted an appendix to it. I make no apology for recording my own views since I know that the situation he found clearly troubled this honourable and decent man. It was therefore necessary for me to explain the complexity and fierceness of the fighting going on around him.

You may wonder why Edgar, in telling his story, dwells at such length on events prior to his joining MI6 in January 1940, before he tells of his wartime exploits – the main subject of this book. He reasoned that it was essential readers should know of the debt he owed to his parents and to his training in the Royal Corps of Signals. His appreciation to his parents and the Royal Signals come in his own words:

'The former, for inculcating into all their ten children such basic values that stood for all time. Discipline, pride in family and country, speaking correctly at all times, and giving service without expectation of earthly reward.

The Royal Signals for its Apprenticeship system that existed at Catterick Camp 1926/38. This enabled boys of 14 to 15 years to become Apprentice Tradesmen, provided they succeeded in passing an examination open to boys of British parentage. The number of places on offer was very limited'

Edgar maintained that his home environment and his army apprenticeship, formed a character able to take on the 'slings and arrows of outrageous fortune' enabling him to achieve so much in the field of communications both in World War II and afterwards.

This is, by any standards, an extraordinary story but the more so because it is a true story. It is about a reserved man from a very humble background who achieved great things for his country and himself. You will read that he first worked in the coalmines of South Wales, then, to better his prospects, sat an examination to join the Army as a boy soldier. This he passed with good results and was one of the few selected for the Royal Corps of Signals as a boy apprentice. In 1929 Edgar thus joined the Army – at the age of 14.

At Whaddon, as well as our bases abroad, those of us in Section VIII were sometimes referred to as 'Toy Soldiers' but here is one who was certainly not. I hope this is a reasonably complete and accurate story of a modest man who was a patriot – as well as a truly fine and brave soldier.

Geoffrey Pidgeon
Richmond
Surrey
September 2008

WINSTON LEONARD SPENCER-CHURCHILL

**He led the United Kingdom to victory in World War II
serving as its Prime Minister from 1940 to 1945**

Whether in London or overseas, Mr. Churchill required to be kept up-to-date with the Bletchley Park output SIGINT and Ultra. When he was abroad, these messages were received by a wireless operator from MI6, included in his entourage.

The operator would be from 'Section VIII' (a division of MI6) responsible for SIS wireless communications. Its main wireless station was at Whaddon Village near Bletchley. The Head of MI6 (Section VIII) was Brigadier Richard Gambier-Parry based in Whaddon Hall.

Edgar Harrison was the chosen wireless operator on several occasions.

Quotes from the Great Man to Edgar.

'You are a remarkable signaller Harrison.'

'What do you mean you *think* you know Harrison?
You either *know*, or you do not *know*!'

Chapter 1

ENERGLYN

Edgar Harrison was born on St David's Day in 1915, the eighth of ten children born to Arthur and Elsie Harrison. He attended the Hendre School at Penyrheol, an adjacent hamlet to Energlyn, from 1919 until 1923. Then boundary changes allowed part of Energlyn to have its education in Caerphilly and this he received at the Gwyndy Boys School in Pontygwyndy Road. The distance from his home to the Gwyndy School was just over a mile, whilst to the Hendre School it was at least two miles so the move was good. He quite enjoyed his schooling.

In 1926 Edgar sat, as was customary, the local Scholarship examination and passed. This entitled him to go to the Grammar School and from then on perhaps to University. 1926 was the year of the General Strike. There was no money to buy the necessary uniform to go to a secondary school and his mother would not go begging to the Parish for money to provide uniforms – so he carried on his schooling at the Gwyndy.

Pupils at Gwyndy Boys' School, Energlyn in South Wales – 1923.
Edgar is second from the right in the middle row.

Now we discover what sparked Edgar's lifelong interest in communication. It was the adjacent huge railway marshalling yard at Energlyn Junction South. Into this yard came locomotives pulling trucks with their loads of coal, iron ore and such like from the different valleys. Quite often he saw a diverse number of railways such as the Rhymney Railway, the Barry Railway, the Taff Railway, the Brecon and Merthyr Railway, the Cardiff Docks Railway, the Great Western Railway and the London North Eastern Railway.

Typical signal box of the period and at a railway marshalling yard – like Energlyn South Junction. Edgar started earning his first wages here by running errands for the signalmen. He was paid the princely sum of five pence a week (£0.025 per week).

The junction was largely controlled by the signal box – Energlyn Junction South – and the signalmen who worked there required someone from time to time to go on errands for them, because obviously they could not leave their box. One Dai Evans, a bachelor who lived in Penyrheol, asked Edgar's father if one of his sons could do it for him, and Edgar duly arrived at the signal box to meet Dai Evans. He regarded Dai Evans as a person who influenced his life just as much as the various masters at school.

Early every morning and before school, Edgar traversed the myriad railway lines to get to the signal box and did whatever jobs Evans required, before he started school. When he returned after school in the evening he repeated the process. For this he was paid the princely sum of five pence a week. Dai Evans gave him three pence a week and his assistant Albert Smith gave him two pence a week. Edgar was now a wage earner.

This way of life carried on from 1926 to 1928 when jobs were so very, very scarce and Edgar was reaching the age when he would have to leave school. Some colliers who worked in the Windsor Colliery at Abertridwr, three miles from Energlyn, required a 'butty'. That is a boy who looks after four or five miners who work at the coalface, enabling them to get on with their work without interference. Edgar's role was to fetch this, carry that, do this, do that! He was offered the job and he jumped at the chance to secure employment at a time when unemployment was at an extremely high level.

The boys underground worked two shifts. There was a morning shift from six until two in the afternoon, and an afternoon shift from two in the afternoon to ten o'clock at night. To enable him to start at six o'clock he needed to get up at four o'clock, walk the three miles to Abertridwr, then go down in the cage to the coalface, do his stint and return home again. That became the daily pattern of his life. He found the colliers robustly kind to him.

Meanwhile, Edgar's father had seen an advertisement in one of the daily papers detailing an Army examination for boys of British parentage – wherever they lived in the world. Successful boys in this examination would secure an apprenticeship in selected corps in the British Army. There were, of course, only a limited amount of vacancies.

Windsor Colliery at Abertridwr. This was a walk of three miles from Edgar's home in Energlyn, where he worked underground in the pit as a 'butty'.

His uncle Edgar provided the five shillings entrance fee and he duly presented himself at Maindy Barracks, Cardiff, the depot of the Welsh Regiment. There, with about twenty other boys, he sat the examination. It consisted of two Maths papers, two English papers and one each of History, Geography and General Knowledge. The whole thing lasted from around half past eight in the morning until about half past four in the afternoon, with a very short midday break. Edgar thought he might have done reasonably well and taking his papers back to the Gwyndy School, found they agreed.

However, he received no notice of results and he carried on working at the Windsor Colliery. Later on, when returning home after a morning shift, he found a letter waiting for him saying he had been successful and that he had come twenty-third – out of all those who sat the examination. Of the 150 apprenticeship places actually on offer, only twelve were allocated to the Royal Corps of Signals.

Edgar – age 14 – was joining the Army!

Chapter 2

APPRENTICESHIP

On 29th April 1929, along with Alfred Roake, a boy from Cardiff, Edgar attested at the depot of the Welsh Regiment at Maindy Barracks at Cardiff. The Adjutant of the Regiment told them to put one hand on the Bible and with the other holding the Union flag, they attested to serve 'Our sovereign and our country' for eight years with the colours, four years in the reserves, plus the time they spent on the apprenticeship course. In Edgar's case, that all added up to a future commitment to military service of sixteen years – and he was not yet fifteen!

Maindy Barracks – Cardiff where Edgar was attested.

That evening, issued with railway tickets at the old Cardiff General Station that read 'Cardiff to Catterick' they commenced an overnight journey, Edgar in short trousers and boots as befitted a young school boy of fourteen at that time. They had to change trains at Crewe, then at Derby, again at York, then finally at Darlington, to catch the train to Richmond (Yorkshire), from where they would go to Catterick Camp.

However, when they arrived at Catterick Bridge the railway inspector appeared, looked at their tickets and said 'You two

Royal Corps of Signals Badge – known as 'Jimmy'.

Edgar with two pals in their early days at Catterick Camp. He sent this to his 'Mam' marked with a cross above to identify himself!

get off here, it says Catterick'. Other people in the compartment – all civilians – told him, 'They are going to Catterick Camp and they have to go on to Richmond'. He replied 'If they want to go on to Richmond, they have to pay extra'. So the pittance they received as subsistence was taken from them to pay to go on to Richmond. At Richmond station, the Railway Transport Officer arranged for transport to come from Catterick Camp and take them to the Signal Training Centre of the Royal Corps of Signals.

The Signal Training Centre consisted of a Depot Battalion, a Mounted Wing, a Dismounted Wing, School of Signals, D Company, E Company and F Company. Edgar was to go to 'F' Company, which was the Boys' Apprentice training company.

There they were fitted out to become soldiers, resourceful, independent and able to take on whatever confronted them. Attributes that Edgar needed in full measure during his extraordinary wartime exploits. Of course, they did the usual 'square bashing' – learning to quick march, slow-march and be competent at the various drills and formations. When that was completed and they passed out, they commenced their training programme proper, which consisted of learning to become 'Operator Signals' and in the future, to become at least senior NCOs in the Royal Corps of Signals.

At the same time, they had their academic education to be looked after and they were expected to attain not less than a first class certificate of education, which would amount to present day 'A' levels. Military instruction went hand in hand with a wide general education.

So, in September 1929, Edgar commenced his training as a communicator and it was this

Boy apprentices queuing for their first issue of sports gear.

Barracks and Mess at Catterick.

schooling that equipped him for his future work in the Army in general and later for his outstanding career in Section VIII of the Secret Intelligence Service, under its brilliant wartime Head – Brigadier Sir Richard Gambier-Parry. But all that was to follow – well in the future!

Operator Signals training at Catterick was initially devoted to learning the Morse code, reaching a speed of upwards of 30 words a minute. To this was added visual telegraphy, the latter using lamps signalling in daylight, plus Helio and flags. This did not take very long and they moved on to line telegraphy, which at that time was confined to use of the

Boys on 'Coal Duty' to shovel the coal being delivered into the bunkers. Seeing how clean they are it was almost certainly taken before the work began. Edgar is second from left.

simplex and duplex sounder board, which enabled them to use it for individual working or duplex working. Having gained expertise in this particular field they were then considered for the next stage, which was the course at Liverpool Post Office.

This course lasted from a year to eighteen months and in Edgar's case it was eighteen months. Arriving there in late 1930, they were accommodated in Seaforth Barracks, the depot of the King's Liverpool Regiment. After breakfast in the Barracks they commuted each day from the Seaforth and Litherland Station to the Exchange Station in Liverpool, then walked to the main Post Office in the city.

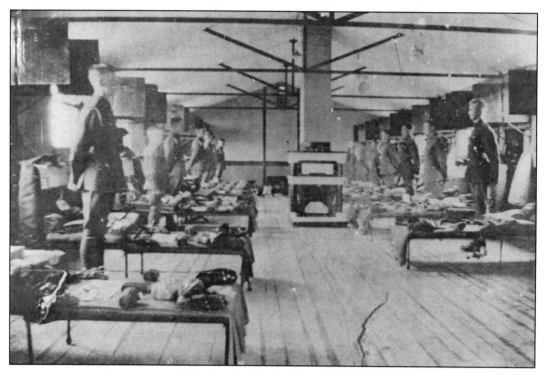

Kit inspection – with every single piece of kit cleaned and in a specific place.

Their main meal of the day was taken at the GPO canteen. At the Training School, they came under the Headmaster and Headmistress of the Post Office Training School. They were exceedingly good at their job. Firstly they taught them how to send and receive correctly, placing great emphasis on the wrist movement and how to handle a key. They then moved on to inker and punching training. The inker was a tape that ran along a cogwheel and recorded the Morse code in dots and dashes.

Similarly with punching, which consisted of a tape that was fed through a small iron contraption containing three metal studs. On the left, one punched in the dots, on the right the dashes, and in the middle was the space button.

So for many months they attained – or struggled to attain – the perfection that the

Headmaster and Headmistress expected of them. When they considered that they were ready to go downstairs to the Instrument Room and be operating live traffic, they had to undergo a test. Here they had to receive 30 telegrams in 30 minutes without error, then to send those same telegrams back – all 30 telegrams in 30 minutes without error. Until they had accomplished this test they were not allowed on a live circuit.

To see fifty operators in the Instrument Room using Sounder machines was indeed an experience. The other part of the Instrument Room was given over to Creed teleprinters that were being gradually introduced and the Baudot system. Already teleprinter circuits were in operation to major cities like London, Dublin, Manchester, Leeds and Cardiff and Baudot to the Baltic countries. This automatic form of sending of telegrams was not in their training programme.

They were confined to the Morse circuits and two circuits in particular tested their expertise to the limit. One was 'Birkenhead B' which dealt exclusively with the cattle market at Birkenhead, where many thousands and thousands of cattle were brought over from Ireland and sold. The Irishmen attending the market then sent back short, pithy telegrams to their villages in Ireland, saying how many beasts they had sold, and what they had been paid for them. The other circuit was to Aintree on Grand National Day when they had anything up to half a dozen circuits to the racecourse. Considering the high volume of money that was exchanged there – it was quite remarkable.

At the same time, they were trained in how to deal with the public with regard to telegraphic traffic, how to ensure that they counted the words correctly, to ensure that they were charged correctly, and very importantly to ensure that there were no 'naughty' words in the telegram.

In this respect, and quoted as the kind of thing they had to worry about, particularly when couples were being congratulated on their marriage, was a particular telegram which read: 'Two pillows trimmed with lace, two lovers face to face, and everything in its proper place. Congratulations.' They had to say that this was not acceptable and this, of course, was way back in 1931.

At the Barracks they were able to indulge in athletics and that included football and boxing. In football, they played the telegraph sections of Liverpool Post Office and clubs of the district, and also the bellboys from the big liners that regularly came into Liverpool Docks. These matches were quite exciting and hard fought.

Boxing was semi-compulsory. Edgar recalled one event where the boxing instructor, a sergeant in the Physical Training Corps, had him in the ring. He was a big man with a big reddish nose. He kept on taunting Edgar, saying, 'Hit me – hit me'.

So suddenly Edgar saw his nose in front of him so he hit it. At the same time he saw the look on the man's face, and he said to himself, Edgar you are for it. So he leaped out of that ring and he was off. He would never have been able to catch Edgar, he was rather quick on his feet!

They were also made to attend church parade, well not exactly church parade, but to go to church at Seaforth every Sunday. It mattered not if they were Church of England or Roman Catholic, everyone had to attend!

Fridays at Liverpool were always special. This was payday and they gave extra special attention to their appearance. The reason for this care was that they were subject to inspection before receiving their pay. First they were looked over by the Headmaster and the Headmistress of the Post Office School, then by their Officer Commanding, a Captain Combe of the Royal Engineers (RE).

Presumably having a Royal Engineer officer in charge stemmed from the time when Royal Signals were part of the Royal Engineers. They had a Boys' unit at Chatham providing communications to the British Army. The Boys were called 'Teleboys' and paid 23 pence a week. Not until 1920 did they become the first Royal Signals Boys' Unit called 'K' company, which in 1925-26 became the famed 'F' Company at Catterick. Edgar was always proud to have been a member of this famous Company.

The 'F' Company Boys' pay consisted of money for their daily commuting from Seaforth to Liverpool Exchange station by train, their daily lunch at the Post Office Canteen and their weekly use of Bootle swimming baths. For the latter, they broke their journey at Marsh Lane station. After these deductions there was precious little left for other activities.

The shortage of cash in their pockets led them occasionally to transgress. This usually occurred on a Wednesday or Thursday when they were utterly broke and they dearly wished to watch a particular film at a Seaforth cinema. They used to take their 'civvy boots' (best 'walking-out' boots) and their nickel spurs to a pawnbroker. He would give them the wherewithal for the cinema, and they would redeem their boots and spurs on Fridays.

Every so often whilst at Liverpool, they were sent to the Castle at Chester. The Castle dates from Roman times and has had a long connection with the Army. Its barracks and training facilities were considerably extended in the 1800s and it was the HQ of Western Command of the Army.

The idea of the visit was to ensure that such military training they had received had not been forgotten. It was there that they were taught how to assemble telephone exchanges and to deal with the public on the telephone. This was so that in the event that the Army took over civilian telephone facilities, they would be in a position to offer these services to the general population in addition, of course, to the Army.

This training finally came to an end and Edgar returned to Catterick Camp. He was very sorry to leave Liverpool, but it was time to move on. His arrival back at the Camp coincided with his younger brother, Wallace, who was two years younger than him, arriving there to start his training.

Part of the time that was left between returning from Liverpool and his eighteenth birthday Edgar spent on an equestrian course. Here, they came under Sergeant Major Young, known as 'Snaky' Young, a magnificent horseman who had represented England at the Olympic games. He and his horse called 'Baby' were just wonderful to behold in action. He disciplined them in all equestrian matters – from the care of horses and harness – right through to the 'mucking-out' of stables and so on.

Edgar well recalled his first morning in stables after the horses were led out. There was all the straw and muck around. They were ordered to clean it up. Edgar ventured to say that they didn't have pitchforks. The Sergeant gave him a withering look and said, 'what do you think your hands are for? Get down and scrape it up.' There and then, they were brought very much down to earth.

Still, they rode and they jumped. Then came the great day when they passed out. This involved doing various intricate movements with the horse and the final hurdle of going down a lane involving jumps including a solid wall. They had to do this with tied reins and stirrups crossed to show that they had complete control of their horses. At the end they had to dismount and to take off the saddle, get the horse to lie down and with a rifle fire at selected targets, so they became quite accomplished horsemen.

Edgar already a trained signalman now masters the equestrian course.

Following the equestrian course came wireless telegraphy training, which up to now had been ignored at the camp. 'F' Company was part of a radio link with Bere Island, Spike Island, Pembroke Dock and Catterick. With a 500 Watt transmitter, they exchanged traffic around this group. It was a strange experience dealing with wireless telegraphy. Edgar took to it in a big way and found it very interesting. In due time, he passed out and received his third class certificate in Operator Signals, which is the highest one could attain at the age of eighteen.

At about this time there was a clamour by the padre for augmentation to his choir – because traditionally 'F' Company Boys provided almost all of the choral part of

St. Martin's Church services. Edgar had not been interested up until then, but he discovered that one received two extra days' leave at Christmas – if one participated. So he became a choirboy, not a very good one, but he became a choirboy. So his boy's service ended.

Except, he could say that in sport in 1932 at Scotton he performed well enough at the Games there to be chosen to represent the Corps at the Northern Command Games. He had participated in the 4 x 100 yards relay and the long jump and he was chosen for these two events and in due course he was presented with his 'Jimmy' of which he remained ever proud. Also at Scotton in 1932 he set an Army junior long jump record. By the way – 'Jimmy' is the nickname given by members of the Royal Corps of Signals to their regimental badge.

A Passing Out Parade taking place on King George V's Birthday.

Chapter 3

TIDWORTH

Edgar's first posting from Catterick was to Armoured Fighting Vehicles depot at Tidworth in Hampshire. So with his kitbag, he set out to walk down and catch the bus to Darlington for the train to take him to London and on to Tidworth. However, the then Commanding Officer, Captain V.C. Holland, known as 'Duchy' Holland, pulled up alongside him in his car and said, 'Jump in Harrison, I'll take you to Darlington.'

As they were going along he asked if Edgar was aware that each year a boy was singled out of the apprentices who they thought might accomplish something in the future. Edgar replied that he knew that to be the case, but as he had not been a very good soldier, in fact he had transgressed on so many occasions, he had not even considered it. However, as they arrived at Darlington, Captain Holland said, 'I would like you to know that I have chosen you for the year 1933.' Edgar was flabbergasted.

So, he went to the Armoured Fighting Vehicles unit at Tidworth. Edgar travelled by train from Darlington to London, then across to Waterloo to catch the Salisbury train. He got out at Andover and changed for Tidworth via Ludgershall. He liked Tidworth, but he remained with Armoured Fighting Vehicles for only a short while as a holding place, before his transfer to 'F' Troop Cavalry Division Signals, attached to the 11th Hussars PAO (Prince Albert's Own). They, together with the 12th Lancers, were the first cavalry regiments to be mechanised.

A Rolls Royce armoured car of the 11th Hussars based at Tidworth – on manoeuvres in the Salisbury area

Edgar's work there was as wireless-operator-gunner in the Squadron Leader's armoured car. There were four squadrons, A, B, and C Squadrons plus the Regimental Headquarter Squadron (RHQ). He remembered the squadron commanders: A Squadron was Major Paul; B Squadron was commanded by Major Combe (of the London brewing company of Watney, Combe & Reid); the Duke of Gloucester commanded C Squadron and Peter Payne-Galway – the RHQ Squadron. Edgar had no experience of gunnery, so to remedy that they sent him to Bovington for a course with the Royal Tank Corps to acquire the skills. So, he was now a wireless-operator-gunner with the 11th Hussars.

The 11th Hussars at their base at Tidworth just prior to going on manoeuvres. The cars in the foreground are 'Austin 7s'. The armoured cars are Lanchesters. It is possible that Edgar is amongst those in the background.

Now Edgar was introduced to another form of communication – radiotelephony. This was because their sets, known as 'MB sets' could work by Morse and also by speech. When the armoured cars were fairly close to each other, say within two or three miles, radio telephony was good and could be guaranteed, whether they were stationary or mobile. But when some armoured cars roamed further afield they required Morse. Then they would, at times, come under the control of the Regimental Headquarters Squadron – RHQ.

RHQ Squadron carried a much larger wireless set and was able to control the four squadrons quite easily. The 11th Hussars had some unusual manoeuvres, or so-called manoeuvres. He recalled one of them. They were on manoeuvres and their Squadron Commander was sent up north with the intention of trying to move south and break through a defensive line, shielding Headquarters at Wilton near Salisbury. They went to somewhere near Leeds, as Edgar recalled, when the Squadron Commander said they were going to paint the wireless van completely white. He gave them all a cap, which read 'Wall's ice-cream – Stop me and buy one'. With this van they penetrated all the lines, and finally captured the HQ at Wilton. However, the referee said that they had cheated and declared their escapade illegal.

RHQ Squadron went up to Aintree for their manoeuvres because its Commander, Peter Payne-Galway, a magnificent horseman, was riding in the Grand National. So why not take his squadron up and let them all enjoy it? Such was the spirit of that wonderful regiment.

The sister regiment, the 12th Lancers, were in Egypt and so a change-about arose when the 11th went to Egypt and the 12th Lancers came home to Tidworth.

This was some time between 1933 and 1936. It came as no surprise to Edgar to learn how well the 11th Hussars performed in the Western Desert in World War II. In fact, Edgar went as far as to say that they probably performed better than any other regiment in that campaign – but one might say he was biased!

The badge of the 11th Hussars.

Chapter 4

CHINA 1933-1938

Whilst at Tidworth, Edgar had passed his B2 examination for Operator Signals with a certain amount of ease. Then, when a form came round asking if they would like to volunteer for service abroad he said he would. So, together with two other ex-apprentice boys also with him at Tidworth, John Graham and Rick Dempsey, they put their names down for the China station and surprisingly their wish was granted. So in late 1933, on the good ship Dorchester, they left for a port called Chinwangtao, which is north of Tientsin. Captain Holland kindly came to see Dempsey, Graham and Edgar off and to wish them well.

Edgar had never been on a ship before. It came as no surprise that he was terribly seasick when they hit very bad weather in the Bay of Biscay. He remained in this state for far too long and but for the ministrations of Graham and Dempsey, he didn't know what might have happened. Anyway, they helped him up on deck by the time they arrived at Gibraltar and from then onwards all was well.

They called in at Malta and Port Said, and going through the Suez Canal was a wonderful experience. At that time, the officers and wives on board used to leave the ship at Port Said, catch the train to Cairo, have a look around Cairo, then on to Port Suez where they rejoined the others. From there, they went to Port Sudan where they discharged the Battalion that they had on ship, whose name he did not recall. However, they embarked the Royal Enniskillen Fusiliers to take them on to Karachi. The Enniskillen

A ship passing through the Suez Canal.

Fusiliers were a strange crowd; they were in part wild Irishmen and in part, extremely affable and friendly. They used to go up on deck singing revolutionary songs like 'The men who killed the Black and Tans came from County Cork' – one song Edgar remembered.

They stopped for a day at Aden and there he discovered how relatively inexpensive things were. T-shirts for example were so cheap, he bought half a dozen and these kept him going until they reached Shanghai. As a result he didn't have to bother too much about the laundering, as this was difficult at any time on board. Actually, Edgar always used the army expression – 'dhobying' – for laundering. In Hindi, 'dhobi' is the word for laundry, and laundry man is a 'Dhobi wallah'.

Arriving at Karachi, they met other ex-apprentice boys from the large signals contingent based there – 'B Corps Signals'. They were staying in the port for some time, as they had to discharge the Royal Enniskillen Fusiliers and take on the Worcester Regiment for onward passage to Chinwangtao. It was enjoyable and he especially recalled the excellent food.

After Karachi they went on to Colombo. There they stayed for a day where Edgar remembered a persistent fortune-teller who kept on hassling him. In the end, he said he would tell Edgar's fortune for nothing. So Edgar held out his hand and he told him he would not have great luck in the monetary sense in his life, but whatever he did obtain, he would have earned it.

The next stop was Singapore where they stayed for a couple of days. Then on to Shanghai, where he saw truly abject poverty for the first time in his life. He thought he had seen poor people earlier in Egypt and again in Aden. It was awful to see these poor people scrabbling for the bilge that came out of the ship, finding bits and pieces and fighting over them. It was truly shocking to him.

From there they went to Chinwangtao, which is an ice-free port in the Bay of Chihli. As there were so few of them compared with the Worcestershire Regiment, they were taken off the ship first and caught the train to Tientsin. Edgar had no knowledge of what the Chinese railway system was like and so it amazed him when they travelled in such luxury, first class travel, and nice food all the way to Tientsin.

There they were met by members of the Tientsin Signal Section who, during the few days they were there, arranged for their uniform to be tailored properly, so that they were a credit to the Corps, before going onwards to Peking, their final destination.

The British Legation in Peking in the 1930s.

At Peking, they were met by Sergeant Teddy Newmarsh, who said they were to become members of the Foreign Office wireless telegraphy station with the call sign HX8. The Royal Navy had built this station in 1931 but having completed the work they then refused to man it. The posts of operators for the station were circulated in the press, in the hope it would attract civilians to man it. A few came along but soon left, as they were not satisfied with the conditions; most particularly they did not like the term of service being a minimum period of three years.

The Army was approached and ex-boy apprentice tradesmen from 'F' Company manned the station from then on, almost exclusively. So when Edgar arrived at the wireless station all the faces were familiar to him from his days in 'F' Company.

Prior to HX8, diplomatic and consular wireless traffic from Tientsin, Shanghai, Peking, Nanking, Hankow and so on, had been transmitted to London from Royal Navy ship to Royal Navy ship, eventually reaching Hong Kong. Then relayed on to Singapore, then to Colombo, and from Colombo along to Aden or Malta, and finally to the United Kingdom.

The transmitter in the diplomatic wireless room, within the British Legation. Installed by the Royal Navy having been taken from the first RMS Mauretania in 1931.

This was a long route and clearly not satisfactory. So the new station HX8, was set in being as a control station communicating with Singapore, Hong Kong, Changsha, Ichang, Chungking, Nanking and Shanghai. It also connected to Rear-Admiral Yangtse, the Royal Naval establishment there, and the C-in-C Far East Fleet, whose call sign was KG.

The HX8 station was housed in the Diplomatic part of His Britannic Majesty's Legation. They took telegraphic traffic from the Consulates in this group from 8 o'clock in the morning to 8 o'clock at night and passed it for processing to the Chancery. They returned traffic to the group until 8 o'clock at night. Meanwhile, the traffic for London was taped up ready for transmission there directly during the night – from 8pm to 8am. The actual transmitters were at a station some 400 yards distant.

There they had one operator whose job it was to get the

One of Edgar's colleagues 'on air'.

transmitters up, shut them off and change frequency when necessary, the job was called the 'conning job'. Incidentally, Edgar explained, the enormous Legation was in two parts. One held the Diplomatic sections (which included their station HX8) and the other housed a Company of the Worcestershire Regiment, which rotated with two other Companies based at Tientsin.

Before going to Peking, the only telegraph procedures Edgar knew were those used by the Post Office and the Army. The latter was similar to that used by the Navy and incorporated 'X' numbers for example, X112 for interrogative. At the Peking Foreign Office Wireless Telegraph Station (FO W/T), the code used to London (Barnes), was the commercial 'Z' procedures.

So the circuit opened with Peking transmitting **GIK 'de' HX8**. 'GIK' being the Rugby transmitter (then being used by Barnes in London) 'de' (from) HX8 the call sign of Peking. This would be followed by 'ZHC' (how are you receiving me?) and then the amount and description of what traffic awaited transmission e.g. ZSC (the letter code), Figs (for figures), cipher and en clair for plain language. Contact having being established all telegrams would be passed expeditiously.

They also communicated, using the 'Q' code, with troopships as required.

From time to time the ex-apprentice tradesmen spoke to Dr. Aspland, the Legation doctor. He had been the doctor during the siege of the Legation by the 'Boxers' ("Harmonious Fists") in the Boxer rebellion.

The Boxers were a loose confederation of anti-foreign Chinese elements; in particular they disliked the Christian Missionaries. The siege lasted 50 days in 1900 until an International relief force arrived when the siege was lifted and the Boxers conquered.

Looking back Edgar thought they should have paid more attention to the stories the Doctor told. In particular, they should have learned more about the 'Lest we Forget Gate' – an underground tunnel where British troops fought to the bitter end to keep the Boxers at bay.

Edgar's stay coincided with the Abdication crisis. They dealt with so many telegrams from the Tongs (great trading establishments in the Orient). All began with the words 'Humble Duty' and without exception deplored Edward VIII's proposed marriage. Such telegrams were, of course, transmitted to London.

Edgar also records, that in addition to the Foreign Office station at Peking, in the military part of the Legation there was a signal station operating a landline to Tientsin. Three or four signalmen, plus a linesman maintained this station. The linesman's job was to ensure that the line from Peking to Tientsin was kept in good order. Frequently, the Chinese would snip a few yards out for a washing line or something of the sort, so the linesman with one or two signalmen, would go on horseback along the line to check. Half the line was the responsibility of Peking, the other half of the line was the responsibility of Tientsin.

The Peking Signals section in Peking – dressed for winter. Edgar standing far right.

In addition to the Consular and Diplomatic traffic handled by HX8 there was another task performed at the station. This was covert work and included intercepting Japanese wireless traffic. Edgar was not closely involved with this traffic at the time. When they arrived, the signalman responsible was 'Titch' Metcalfe, an ex-boy from Catterick and John Graham took over this duty. Edgar did not know what was wrong but clearly John Graham could not cope with the work and it affected his mind.

He was not told the full story but they had apparently managed to prevent Graham from climbing over the wall into the Japanese Legation. Nobody knew what he intended to do there but he was clearly mentally disturbed and he was put in the British Legation hospital for a time. While he was there, they took it in turns to walk him round the grounds, as also did Sir Alexander and Lady Cadogan's daughter, Patricia. Alexander Cadogan was our Minister Extraordinary and Plenipotentiary in Peking.

On Graham's departure to hospital, Edgar was asked if he would carry on his work. Not having had any training in the field he was stumped at first, but says 'eventually I got the hang of it'. Then Captain Phillips, the assistant Military Attaché came over and said that the work he was producing was good and to stick at it. Edgar was intrigued, because he could not understand that the Japanese station – which he presumed was in Tokyo and used the call sign R7F – came up at regular times of the day with a traffic statement giving the call signs of lots of stations. Having sent the traffic blind, as they said, R7F closed down and that was that!

What intrigued Edgar was, surely the out-stations must have had some queries on the traffic; what happened when they had traffic, to whom did they send it and how? He first tackled the Japanese station next door to their Legation and he quickly found out that it was acknowledging traffic, sending traffic, and obviously getting receipts for it.

Over the course of many months he plotted the whole of the covert Japanese diplomatic wireless service, and this gave him much pleasure, as it necessitated a great deal of travelling across the region.

In fact, he reports going to Inner Mongolia, Outer Mongolia (where he visited Ulan Bator), Manchuria, Korea, Sinkiang, Tibet, Hong Kong. He lists visiting Siberia but whether he just crossed the borders into the country or spent any time there, is not recorded. However, these excursions, perhaps supported by study back in Peking, were how Edgar picked up his understanding of Russian that subsequently helped him when he was in Russia. Clearly, his work on the Japanese networks was highly confidential and important to the Foreign Office at the time.

The Great Wall of China.
Edgar tells of riding along part of it.

For Edgar, it was rewarding and he was happy and contented with his achievements. Unfortunately for us, he does not describe how he travelled over such a large region. However, knowing his life-long love of railways that was probably how most of it was achieved.

Those in charge of the covert work at the Embassy would have paid for his extensive travel as well as his accommodation. In addition – because of the excellent work he was doing for 'them' – he would certainly have been in receipt of a generous allowance. Nonetheless, he records that at times, in the more remote areas, he lived amongst the local population and was treated as an honoured guest and occasionally given a fish head with his rice!

In his spare time back in Peking, he felt able to get out and about with ease. He regularly made trips to the Imperial Palace, Nan Hai, Bei Hai, Temple of Heaven and Temple of Earth.

However, his most memorable visit was to the Summer Palace on the outskirts of the city. He travelled there by tram and rickshaw. Although steps had been taken to restore it to its former glory and were on going, still much needed to be done. He asked a Chinese guide to translate some of the Chinese characters on a column. He was familiar with a number of them (of which there are something like 40,000) because for every 100 learnt he received a few pence more in pay. Literacy requires knowledge of about 2000.

A corner of the Summer Palace in Peking that so impressed Edgar.

It was embarrassing for him to be told how General Gordon had allowed his troops to pillage and loot the temple. Although he knew it was common at one time for a General to allow twenty-four hours of pillage, he felt quite ashamed.

However, there were occasions when the odd incident gave him cause to smile. In 1935 part of the Legation was given its first sewage system. The construction involved the digging of a trench across the field they crossed to reach their W/T station. He noticed, that of the gang of twenty or so labourers digging the trench, a solitary worker was some distance from the main party. Edgar enquired of the foreman, why? 'Da fung la,' he replied. This Edgar interpreted as 'fire in the head'. The solitary worker was a redhead. They thought he must be somewhat mad. Subsequently Edgar noticed that when a pal 'Ginger' Cann (obviously a redhead), accompanied them to the cinema or restaurant, there was a marked reluctance by the Chinese cashiers to take money for his ticket or his bill.

He used to go into Peking itself and there were two restaurants and a YMCA, which they frequented. The restaurants were Hempels and Karactus. Germans ran Hempels, whereas Karactus was Russian and the YMCA was run by volunteers.

Anyway, it was at the YMCA one day that he saw this most beautiful girl. She was the product of an American mother and a Chinese father, who were both doctors at the Peking Union Medical College. He was smitten, there was no better word for it and it became very obvious to all. So obvious, that out of the blue he was told that he would be sent away and he was posted to Tientsin. He was so very sorry to leave Peking, but there it was. The year was 1937.

Arriving at Tientsin, there were quite a few ex-apprentice boys and also George Sommerfield, who had come up from Hong Kong with two signalmen to take over at Tientsin, the work that Edgar had been doing in Peking.

The Royal Signals at Tientsin, were part of the 'Staff and Departmentals' consisting of small numbers of personnel belonging to the Royal Engineers, Royal Army Service Corps and Royal Army Ordnance Corps, in addition to the signalmen. In all they numbered about twenty-five. This number included two corporals and two lance corporals.

Their quarters were good; infinitely better in every way compared with Peking. They had their own dormitory with attached bathroom and toilets. Their Mess consisted of a large lounge and dining room with well-equipped kitchen. They took it in turn to accompany their cook to the markets to purchase all the food for their meals. Additionally, at regular intervals, a 56-gallon barrel of beer would arrive by sea from Scotland and the sale of this beer helped with the Mess finances.

This was without doubt the best accommodation and food Edgar enjoyed during his years in China. His rate of pay enabled him to have his own rickshaw and puller to take him to and from the Signals Office and his quarters. A signalman with all his qualifications earned almost the same as a sergeant in an infantry regiment.

Edgar broke off here to mention a little of the signals activities in Tientsin. Tientsin was part of a circuit, controlled from Hong Kong with the call sign LOA. Tientsin's call was VBA and Shanghai's signal section call was POA. During the summer months, when part of the Regiment moved to Shanhaikuan on the Manchurian border, that became QBA and the signalmen took it in turn to man this station and this was considered their holiday.

Now this was the only time off – or so-called holiday – that any signalman in North China enjoyed. It was a working holiday, but it was a nice posting to Shanhaikuan. He certainly enjoyed the odd occasions that he went there. The first time was from Peking when he went with Graham and Dempsey. There they found horses, or griffins as they were called, were freely available at a very cheap rate and they used to go riding.

He recalled one particular day they were riding along the Great Wall, which ends at the sea at Shanhaikuan. As they were riding along they passed the Japanese encampment and there was an enormous crowd there. They had no idea what it was about but something

made them laugh. Suddenly they were surrounded and he understood that they were guilty of great disrespect. He was told it was Emperor Meiji's birthday or something of the sort. Anyway, they had to kow-tow and humbly beg forgiveness before they were allowed to ride on. A kow-tow was a sign of submission when the forehead had to touch the ground. Fortunately Edgar was very fit in those days!

A mule drawn 'railway' used to take men and supplies from Shanhaikuan station to their 'Holiday camp' three miles away.

The holiday camp at Shanhaikuan was about three miles from Shanhaikuan railway station and between the camp and station there had been constructed a light railway, which carried containers pulled by mules and took personnel and goods up and down.

Their responsibility was to maintain a telegraph line from the camp to the stationmaster at Shanhaikuan to acquaint him with the number of people who were travelling and such like. This line was frequently broken so they travelled up and down the line mending it as needed.

Back to Tientsin. Sport was plentiful as compared with Peking. He mentioned that in much of this they vied with Tientsin Grammar School whose Headmaster was the missionary, Dr. Liddell – he of 'Chariots of Fire' fame. He would have been about 40 years old but with his bald-pate, appeared older. He was a great competitor participating in most games and athletics.

However, there was nothing to test Edgar's skills in communications in Tientsin but amongst the staff was a 'Foreman of Signals' who was competent and qualified to test him for the highest trade certificate possible – a B Class 1. He sat and attained the certificate so now he had the highest certificates possible in both his trade and education. You would have thought that entitled him to promotion. Not a bit of it.

On reflection, his lack of promotion was not surprising since one of his reports said he was the worst of soldiers but the best of technicians! Certainly, he did not easily accept discipline, if he thought it unfair, or unwarranted.

He did not like being on a station and not working. Whilst he had been able to operate an amateur radio station in Peking with Dempsey, and construct various pieces of equipment which they used to experiment with around the Legations, nothing like that was available in Tientsin. When the opportunity arose and an ex-boy in Shanghai, Paddy Boyd, expressed a desire to serve in North China, Edgar said he would transfer and so in 1937 he arrived at Shanghai Signal Section at Tifeng Road, at the top end of Bubblingwell Road in Shanghai.

Shanghai was very different indeed. Here was an enormous city, absolutely modern, offering anything or everything – provided of course one had the money. They were, as Edgar has previously said, part of the army wireless link, Hong Kong, Shanghai, Tientsin.

Now Shanghai was no stranger to war. In the 1930s there had been very severe problems, which were only suppressed by the sending of a fair number of troops plus the so-called Shanghai Volunteer Corps. The Shanghai Volunteer Corps was comprised almost entirely of Russians, very fine soldiers and an excellent fighting force. These came under Brigadier Telfor-Smollett who commanded all the British troops in Shanghai.

At the time Edgar was there the Second Battalion of the Loyal Regiment of Lancashire was in residence. Whilst they were not based at Tifeng Road, where the Signals had their station, they used to see members of the 'Loyals' from time to time.

He discovered Shanghai was a free city and very different from those he had served in before. The Chinese authorities designated certain areas outside the old city for foreign use. The British and American merged into the International Settlement whilst the French continued as an extension of the French colonial government in Hanoi and became the French Concession.

Traders from many companies were attracted to the port from the mid-19th century and the Japanese joined them later that century. Their area was in Hongkew which was over the Soochow Creek and where the International Post Office was situated.

Edgar had his second skirmish with the Japanese there as they had control of the bridge he had to cross to reach the Post Office on the mail run. It was necessary to take a certificate to show one had all the required inoculations against diseases. On this day he forgot his certificate and the Japanese doctor would not take his word that he had had all the inoculations. Instead the doctor immediately got hold of his syringes with the idea of inoculating him.

The Signals Section in Shanghai 1937. Edgar is standing 6th from the right.

Winners of the Tsz Ling Cup 1937. Edgar, star of the match is standing second from left.

Edgar would have none of that and pushed him away. In no time he found himself in a Japanese prison cell and there he remained until he had kow-towed – full of apologies. Needless to say, he did not forget the medical certificate again.

They did various wireless exercises in Shanghai, and he was able to extend his knowledge of amateur wireless. In fact, he had two stations there XU2VW and XU2VZ, and having made his own transmitter and receiver, he was proud that he could get an output of something like 5 watts with a tune-plate, tune-grid transmitter TPTG. With this he managed to secure the coveted certificate of contacting all Continents.

There was one great day when round about 2 o'clock in the morning he was hopefully sending out a CQ, which means to all stations, when lo and behold he had a reply from somebody in Manchester. It did not seem possible that there he was with this tiny transmitter talking to him. It was, Edgar thought, the greatest moment in his life in amateur wireless.

There was the great occasion of the Coronation Tattoo – in honour of the Coronation at Westminster of King George VI – that was held on the racecourse in the centre of the city. The signallers operated the all-important lighting. He still had a copy of the commemorative programme of this grand spectacle. Apart from British troops and the Shanghai Volunteer Force (SVF) the Americans, yes the Americans, made a significant contribution to this three-day affair.

Mention must also be made of the famous victory by the 'Area Details' soccer team over the fancied champion Chinese side. The latter were expected to win handsomely, and should have done. They did not take their chances but Edgar's side made the most of theirs. His fluke goal in the dying moments of the game saw the 'Tsz Ling' Cup in their hands. The headlines in Shanghai's leading sports paper the following day read – *'Harrison's fluke goal secures a highly improbable victory!'*

Whilst Edgar was in Peking, Tientsin and Shanghai, the Japanese were making increasing encroachments into China. Having already subjugated Manchuria where they set up a puppet state in 1931, they encroached on other parts of North China.

The 'incidents' continued. The Japanese seized on a small incident at the Marco Polo Bridge at Wan-p'ing southwest of Peking on 7th July 1937 and thereafter a de-facto state of war existed between the might of the Japanese Imperial Army and Chiang Kai-Shek's

Severe damage and heavy casualties were caused in the city of Shanghai during the Japanese attacks in 1937.

Nationalist forces. Shanghai was threatened and Chiang Kai-Shek mobilised his forces in the Chinese quarter of the City

At first the foreign settlements and concessions were not involved but in August 1937 a Chinese pilot mistakenly dropped bombs on the Bund and on an area including an entertainment complex. As a result, over 1000 were killed and a similar number injured. The Japanese had assembled numerous warships at Shanghai and were firing over the British positions to Chinese army positions and the Chinese were replying in kind. Not all the shells reached their intended target. Life was not very easy at Tifeng Road as they could hear the shells screaming overhead.

Then Edgar was told that the section would employ wireless sets to provide communications with certain interests outside Shanghai, but the only sets they had in store were known as the 'A Set'. When these sets were produced it was found that apart from Edgar, no one had any idea how to operate them. Over and over again, they carried out wireless exercises, and eventually out they went. Edgar went with Signalman Shannon to the Toyata Mills – but he had no idea why they were sent there.

They exchanged signals and they were then under heavy fire, with one shell landing in the courtyard. All he remembered of that shell was that the pieces of it were so hot that he decided 'we have to get out of here – fast!'

Later the signal came that they could leave and it was very hairy indeed. During this time there were many casualties and British soldiers were being buried at Bubblingwell Road Cemetery. It was not, as has been said, a very nice time to be in China. The British and American governments began to scale back their military presence.

Eventually, the day came to leave Shanghai for home. However, one last pleasant memory came to mind about the place. One evening Edgar went to the equivalent of the Union Jack Club in the centre of Shanghai. He had just two Chinese dollars in his

Hearse taking some of the British Army soldiers killed in the Japanese attack, to the Bubblingwell Cemetery.

Troops lining the route to the Bubblingwell Cemetery.

pocket and decided to chance his luck at 'Housie Housie' (Tombola). He won almost every 'House' and became embarrassed collecting his winnings. His luck was really in.

He went to watch the game of 'Hi Ali' (a game introduced by the Portuguese?). Anyway, he decided to wager on a player named 'Bilbao the Second'. He had yet to win a match during two years playing in Shanghai. The odds were long, Bilbao won and Edgar returned to Tifeng Road a rich man. What to do on Sunday? Well as his luck was in, he decided to go to the racecourse and back the horses. He picked the winner in the first race and then lost everything on the subsequent races. Afterwards he said – there is a moral lesson for us all there somewhere!

(Appendix 4 has comments on the Sino-Japanese war.)

Chapter 5

HOME SERVICE 1938-1939

Now, homeward bound in 1938 and he had more real luck. On the way out to China in 1933, he had been of some assistance to the wireless operators on board because of his knowledge of wireless telegraphy. So when he stepped on board the Dilwara at Shanghai to return home, one of the operators remembered him and he spent his entire voyage as part of the wireless operating team on the ship. He had wonderful food and a nice place to sleep. It was very good indeed.

They stopped off at the usual places en-route and eventually arrived at Southampton where he was informed that he had been posted to the 3rd Divisional Signals at Bulford.

While in Tidworth Camp back in 1933, he had had a bad attack of quinsy that put him in hospital for a few days. He recovered but it was not a very pleasant experience. However, in Peking he was struck down with it again. He believed it was hereditary because his mother suffered from it. It was so bad at Peking that a telegram was sent home saying he was seriously ill. In Shanghai things got much worse and he had a very bad attack again. This is a most unpleasant illness.

A telegram was sent to his parents saying he was dangerously ill. He recovered but a recommendation was made, that as soon as he arrived in the United Kingdom, he should get in touch with the Army medical section and explain that he needed a tonsillectomy, as soon as possible. So arriving at Bulford he went on 28 days leave, then went back to Tidworth and into the hospital there. He had his tonsils out and he claims he was 'as right as rain' thereafter.

So, back to 3rd Divisional Signals. This unit was famed throughout the pre-war Army for its prowess at athletics, having a number of army champions and the like. So it came about Edgar was ordered to report at the playing fields of Bulford. He had been selected for sprinting, jumping and similar events. He was annoyed about it and he demanded to see the Commanding Officer.

Edgar explained that he saw his future in communications and not in athletics and he should like to be transferred to another unit. So, very quickly he found himself on the way to 2nd Divisional Signals at Aldershot. It was there that he was able, as part of a signal section, to further his communication skills with the Guards Brigade signal section, and Artillery Brigade signal section. This all proved excellent in preparing him for the future.

Almost immediately after he arrived at 2nd Divisional Signals, he was selected to go to Bristol Post Office on a teleprinter-operating course and to learn about maintaining teleprinter machines. Having had some experience at Liverpool Post Office he really enjoyed the work. Now, as a result of his training at Bristol he became skilled at mechanical methods of communication, so he returned to Aldershot with flying colours. His CO wrote 'I sent him to Bristol on a course and he disappointed me – he came top.'

Someone saw to it that Edgar was actually promoted to 'acting-unpaid-lance corporal'. He held this 'rank' for a short while, when he and another ex-boy, 'Ginger' Cann, who had also been promoted the same as Edgar, were called to the CO and he said 'I am making you paid lance corporals established immediately.'

He then said, 'I should like you to agree that instead of having your four years on the reserve, you actually sign on for the additional four years.' They asked for a little time to consider it and he agreed. They later returned and told him that – provided he promoted them to full corporal on full corporal's pay they would do it – and he accepted.

Thus it was as a full corporal, that Edgar found himself posted back to Catterick, as an Instructor in the Operators Training Battalion, which also incorporated the Officer Cadet Training Unit. He liked the work there and enjoyed his position. He had a car, so he was quite mobile and he had more money than he had ever had before. And in addition, he had a good friend with him, Stanley Bristow, another ex-apprentice boy.

Edgar Harrison is promoted Corporal on full Corporal's pay – in exchange for signing on for four years with the colours – instead of being on the reserve for that time.

Chapter 6

EDGAR'S INTRODUCTION TO MI6 – SECTION VIII

This was 1939 and war was looming. In the September, whilst Edgar was at Catterick, war was declared against Germany and training became more and more intense. Then, in January 1940, right out of the blue, he was told to report to the Orderly Room. Reporting there, he was told that he should proceed to St. John's Wood Barracks in London as early as possible. When he asked why, they said they had no idea; all they knew was that it was his name on the movement order, his army number, and his rank, so it had to be Edgar who had been instructed to go! So off he went to London by train. He arrived at the Barracks, reported in and asked what he had to do. They said they did not know but he would receive instructions the next day and meantime not to unpack.

The next morning he was told to go to Euston Station and call at the RTO (Rail Transport Officer), who would give him his instructions. He arrived and was given a sealed envelope and the RTO told him to catch the train going to Northampton and Rugby. When he was inside the train – and only then – he was to open the envelope. As the train started Edgar opened it and the note enclosed read: *'You will alight when you get to Bletchley Station and on the platform will be somebody whom you will recognise and he will know you.'*

So it came about that Charles Emary, who again was an ex-'F Company' boy but some two and a half years his senior, met him at Bletchley Station. Although he was in civilian clothes, he said he was a Lieutenant in a unit headed by Colonel Richard Gambier-Parry, and he took Edgar to nearby Bletchley Park. He was asked if he had civilian clothes and was told to put them on. They then went to what was known as the 'Big House' – the Mansion – at Bletchley Park. Here, in their offices, he was made a member of

Bletchley Park Mansion that Edgar described as 'The Big House' on joining MI6 (Section VIII) in January 1940.

MI6 (Section VIII) and found that he was to be paid by MI6 and no longer by the Army. Quite apart from anything else, it was a considerable increase to his income!

Richard Gambier-Parry was Head of MI6 (Section VIII), the organisation handling communications for SIS. He had been the General Sales Manager of Philco, a large American wireless company with extensive manufacturing and research facilities in England. Indeed, Philco was the largest wireless factory in the UK at the time.

The Head of SIS in pre-war years (known to the public only as 'C') was Admiral Sir Hugh Sinclair. It was Sinclair who had purchased Bletchley Park as his 'War Station' so that various departments of SIS would have a safe work place in the event of war. In 1938, he had looked for a man to head up his new communication organisation. Gambier-Parry was chosen, probably proposed by Col. Stewart Menzies, who was then Head of the military wing of MI6 who later, in November 1939, became "C' himself.

Brigadier Richard Gambier-Parry,
Head of MI6 – Section VIII.

Charles Emary told him that, along with one other person, he would be preparing agents to go into Europe. To begin with, he thought Edgar could assist them in the training of a Norwegian agent.

Edgar could not recall the name of the agent but he reports that he was quite good as an operator. As part of the training, it was essential that he knew the signal plans. This signal plan allowed him to change frequency without indication, change times without indication, change code without indication, memorise codes and suchlike. This took a long time to inculcate. Anyway, the training was later continued at Whaddon Hall where Section VIII were being re-housed due to the rapidly increasing pressure on accommodation at Bletchley Park, arising from the rapid growth of GC&CS (Government Code and Cipher School – the 'Codebreakers').

Whaddon Hall became the HQ of MI6 (Section VIII). The Hall is in the little village of Whaddon, about six miles west of Bletchley Park. By that time, Section VIII was handling all SIS communications. The Section VIII wireless equipment fitted in the tower of the Mansion at Bletchley Park, known as 'Station X' and the 'Main Line' wireless station in 'Hut 1' were being dismantled and moved to Whaddon.

Whaddon Hall: The newly acquired HQ of Section VIII and the new home for 'Station X' moved from Bletchley Park. The transfer was completed by March 1940.

Edgar was accommodated in the Dower House, a short way from the Hall itself, and here he met 'Spuggy' Newton, a wireless engineer originally from Newcastle, who later became a very close friend. His Christian name was Arthur but he acquired the nickname of 'Spuggy' but nobody knows how.

He had been the car wireless expert at Philco and recruited by Richard Gambier-Parry from Philco into Section VIII, along with its Chief Designer Bob Hornby, Alf Willis Manager of the Birmingham region, Wilf Lilburn his equivalent in Glasgow and Charlie West. One wonders how Philco managed to operate successfully after losing so many of its most talented men?

Arthur 'Spuggy' Newton a friend of Edgar, taken at Whaddon circa 1943.

However, Edgar also assisted 'Spuggy' in fitting some of the first of the sixty plus Packard motorcars acquired by Gambier-Parry with the latest wireless equipment they had at the time. Bob Hornby and 'Spuggy' Newton had been leading the way into miniaturisation at Philco, to replace the bulky car sets that had been manufactured hitherto.

Looking back, it is interesting that Edgar was involved in those early days in fitting wireless transmitters and receivers to Section VIII vehicles. Earlier two cars had been fitted out and travelled to the British Expeditionary Force in France to receive the Bletchley Park output of SIGINT. In 1941 a unit from Whaddon Hall known as 'A Detachment' was sent to North Africa with several Packards to replicate the success demonstrated by those two early cars in France. However, this time they were to receive the rapidly expanding output of 'Enigma' based traffic coming out from Bletchley Park – via the Windy Ridge wireless station in Whaddon village.

A Packard Sedan (saloon!) from the Packard catalogue for 1940. The unit acquired 60 of this model (and others) from Leonard Williams Ltd – the Packard UK distributor based at Brentford in 1940. Edgar and 'Spuggy' worked on fitting these early SLUs with our wireless gear.

(Appendix 1 gives details about Bletchley Park and Whaddon Hall)

Chapter 7

NORWAY
EDGAR'S FIRST AGENT AND HIS FIRST RETREAT

Life at Whaddon continued fairly uneventfully for a time. Edgar continued to train the Norwegian agent in Morse, the use of their special wireless equipment and procedures. Then came a day when things changed dramatically for them. Edgar was sent by Richard Gambier-Parry up to Scotland with the Norwegian agent to board a waiting destroyer to cross the North Sea and land him in Norway. All the time during the crossing he was coaching the agent in the signal plans and testing him again and again, so that he would know them by heart. Their departure from Scotland coincided with the German invasion of Norway on 9th April 1940. It would seem Richard Gambier-Parry either had previous knowledge of the event through SIS or it was an extraordinary coincidence.

After an uneventful crossing of the North Sea, they arrived in a fjord in northern Norway where Edgar went ashore with the agent, a small party of officers and ratings. However, they found there were a number of Norwegians present who did not appear

Narvik in northern Norway after suffering from heavy German bombing. Edgar's party, in accepting Norwegian orders to leave Norway, avoided becoming involved in the fighting.

Destroyer of the type used by Edgar's party for the visit to Norway.

happy to see them and this surprised Edgar. The Norwegians said yes, they knew the Germans were in their country, but they felt that they would learn how to deal with them. They would be very pleased if Edgar and his Naval party would leave just as fast as they could.

Having put the agent safely ashore with his wireless sets and other equipment, they wished him good luck. Edgar boarded the destroyer and left hastily to return to the Naval base in Scotland. Then, for Edgar, it was back to Whaddon Hall to explain to Richard Gambier-Parry what had happened and to relate to him the story of his first retreat!

German tanks in Oslo as they take control of Norway

(Appendix 2 refers to Richard Gambier-Parry Head of MI6 – Section VIII.)

Chapter 8

BRUSSELS AND HIS SECOND RETREAT
VIA DUNKIRK

By May 1940 Whaddon was a hive of industry with more personnel being recruited to serve the ever-wider roles undertaken by Section VIII. The remaining wireless facilities at Bletchley Park had long since been removed to Whaddon and were in operation. Outstations were being constructed in villages in the surrounding countryside. One of these was 'Nash' just outside the pretty village of Nash some three miles away. It eventually worked wireless traffic to SIS agents in occupied Europe and particularly to agents in France, Belgium and initially Norway.

One day, shortly after his return from Norway, Edgar was told to go as a matter of urgency to Brussels to assist 'Bungy' Williams – the Section VIII operator there who was working the covert traffic in the Embassy – under the Passport Control Officer. The increasing volume of wireless traffic was becoming too much for Williams to handle alone and twenty-four hour coverage had become essential. So off Edgar went to Brussels. Within forty-eight hours they cleared the backlog between them and were able to cope with the heavy and growing flow of messages.

The Passport Control Office in Embassies abroad charged for the issue of visas and passports and it was a simple method of adding to the slim finances of MI6. It was short of funds and neglected in pre-war years – to the point that Admiral Sinclair had actually purchased Bletchley Park with his own money! In most Embassies, the senior SIS officer was known as the Passport Control Officer (or PCO).

Then, out of the blue, came the German attack on Belgium. All was utter chaos. Before lunch they were running a normal station and after lunch they were destroying their codes, wireless equipment, indeed anything likely to be of help to the

Stuka dive bombers were used in large numbers against the Allies.

Germans. 'Bungy' Williams and Edgar then set off, intending to make their way to the coast. It was a most unpleasant journey and they often came under fire from low flying aircraft – strafing the roads. But so many others were certainly in a worse state.

Edgar could not remember where they parted company but he recalled 'Bungy' had the idea of going to Ostend, or somewhere on the coast nearby. Anyway, he decided he was going to go one way, whereas Edgar decided he would take his chances and go the other. This took him to Dunkirk where,

Troops moving through the town of Dunkirk, some of whom were to stay behind and fight a rearguard action to cover their escape.

after enduring considerable difficulties, he was able to get onto a destroyer back to Folkestone and quickly he was returned to Whaddon Hall.

He regarded himself as very fortunate indeed. Not only had he survived his first retreat from Norway but now a second retreat from a Europe being completely overrun by German forces.

Thousands of British troops with French and Belgian soldiers among them, waiting on the beaches to be picked up by ships and little boats in Operation Dynamo.

Troops waiting on the beach for rescue made brave attempts to fight back – even using their rifles!

Looking back on Dunkirk as smoke rises from the bombed-out town; despite constant air attacks by German planes the rescue goes on.

Men, many of whom were standing neck-high in water for hours at a time, eventually being picked up and evacuated back to Britain.

Returning troops being greeted like heros after escaping the horrors of Dunkirk and the disastrous loss of equipment.

On arrival back at Whaddon Hall, he reported in to Gambier-Parry, who told Edgar that he had no news whatsoever of 'Bungy' Williams. In fact, sadly, he must have been lost in the scramble to get out of the way of the German Blitzkrieg. It was suggested he might have been in one of the many ships that left the French or Belgium coast only to be sunk by German aircraft or 'E' Boats. Needless to say, Edgar considered himself to be very lucky.

Whilst he was waiting at Whaddon, he went over to Nash one day and asked Bert Gillis, who was running the station at the time, if there was anything he could do to help. He asked Edgar to listen out for the agent he had taken to Norway, as they had not heard anything from him.

Edgar started listening daily and in time he was absolutely delighted when he contacted him and everyone was pleased that he was safe and in position. They then started to exchange traffic. It was a wonderful feeling for him to make the first contact with an agent he had trained and put into the field.

German soldiers examine a bombed British ship in Dunkirk harbour

Chapter 9

EMERGENCY COMMAND STATION AT CHESTER

Edgar continued to find work to do at Whaddon but the news was grim – with talk of a German invasion in the air. The Cabinet Office had earlier decided that in the event of an invasion, they had to have mobile wireless communication at the military headquarters in various parts of the country, Southern Command at Wilton, Western Command at Chester, Northern Command at York, Scottish Command at Edinburgh, and the Irish Command at Belfast.

These long-established Army Commands were amongst the few military organisations unaffected by the débâcle of the collapse of France and the withdrawal of the remains of the British Expeditionary Force from the Continent. They were now able to act as control points for the reorganisation of the bedraggled forces returning from the Continent, as well as being established centres for intelligence and the other aspects of military organisation.

The ancient Chester Castle partially housed the Western Command, one of the long-established organisations used to coordinate the reassembly of the British Army after Dunkirk.

The concept of mobile communications to pass SIGINT and the earliest Enigma traffic deciphered at Bletchley Park, directly to the HQ of Military Commanders, had already been put into being. The first two vehicles (fitted out by Section VIII engineers at Whaddon), had been sent to the British Expeditionary Force HQ, first to France and then into Belgium. One was certainly fitted into a Dodge car and the second probably into either the unit's Humber or Oldsmobile.

These were the first Signal Liaison Units (SLUs) later referred to by Wing Commander Fred Winterbotham RAF when he wrote his book 'The Ultra Secret'. There is no record of the vehicles returning after the Blitzkrieg but certainly one of the operators did – in the person of Bill Sharpe. No doubt the vehicles were destroyed en-route together with their codes and equipment.

The first step was to establish these mobile units at the major seats of control like the Admiralty, the War Office and Fighter Command. There was obviously concern that enemy bombing could break their newly established teleprinter links with Bletchley Park and thus sever the flow of SIGINT. Another major factor was that these vital commands might have to move northwards – as the anticipated German invasion rolled across the southern counties of England and into London. They clearly needed to have up-to-date intelligence as they moved – hence the mobile units of Section VIII.

Richard Gambier-Parry who had obtained permission and the funds, to purchase a fleet of suitable motor cars for the purpose, had already anticipated this. He chose 'Sedans' (saloons) made by the Packard Automobile Company of America, and purchased the entire stock of current models from their UK distributor Leonard Williams & Co, Limited, based in Brentford in London.

Edgar was sent to Chester in one of our 60 + Packard Sedans fitted out as wireless vehicles or 'SLUs'. This particular Packard is one of 'A Detachment' SLUs intended to handle SIGINT in exactly the same way, but sent to North Africa.

Over a period of time the cars were taken to Whaddon Hall, camouflaged locally at Tickfords factory at Newport Pagnell and then, one by one, fitted with wireless gear. Edgar had been involved with this task – along with other engineers – under the supervision of 'Spuggy' Newton. In July of 1940, Richard Gambier-Parry instructed Edgar to take a Packard wireless car north to Western Command at Chester, set up a station and be responsible for high level intelligence to the Command there.

At Chester, he had sited his station in a field approximately half way between Chester and Eccleston. Eccleston was, of course, where Eaton Hall was situated in the heart of the Duke of Westminster's estate.

Edgar soon had his station operational. They then held some very successful exercises to test the concept of providing local signals intelligence – so vital in the conduct of the war – when the German forces were massed on the French coast. They proved they were able to pass traffic expeditiously from area to area – in the event of an invasion – just as Richard Gambier-Parry had planned.

Chapter 10

MISSION TO GREECE
AND THE THIRD RETREAT

Life continued with routine of maintenance and regular wireless exercises at Chester until late September, when Gambier-Parry arrived with a passenger – introduced to Edgar as Hunter Anderson. He was a fairly dour Scot, Post Office trained, a good operator but very taciturn. He was told Anderson had come to replace him and he was to return to Whaddon that day with Gambier-Parry. They chatted a little on the journey south but as they parted, he told Edgar to see him the following morning.

Brigadier Richard Gambier-Parry (to the left) Head of MI6 (Section VIII) and based at Whaddon Hall sent Edgar Harrison to Greece to provide SIGINT and Ultra traffic directly to his brother Major-General Michael Gambier-Parry (to the right) – Head of the British Military Mission to Greece.

He duly went to Richard Gambier-Parry's office in the Hall as instructed and was told 'For this, I could have sent any one of your colleagues, but I considered that you are the best for this particular task.' He went on to say that, as Edgar probably knew, the Italians had taken Albania and declared war on Greece. His brother, Major-General Michael Gambier-Parry, was Head of the Military Mission in Athens and required secure wireless communications as a matter of urgency.

Equipment for a full wireless station and operations in the area had been assembled. Having worked at Whaddon Hall with agents and in the Whaddon workshops, Edgar knew the fittings selected for him quite well by that time. He was told he was to be flown out to Athens. When he asked when he would be leaving, Gambier-Parry said 'tomorrow' and when asked for how long, Gambier-Parry said 'no longer than six months.' So, Edgar rapidly packed his personal gear and was told the plane would be leaving from Pembroke Dock but this was subsequently changed to Plymouth. When he arrived at the port he found there was a Sunderland flying boat waiting. He put all the equipment aboard and late at night they set off for their first call – Gibraltar.

A Sunderland flying boat as used to fly Edgar and his wireless gear to Greece. For the flight across the Mediterranean he acted as one of its air-gunners.

Arriving at Gibraltar, they stayed there for a day and a half. A VIP had to be taken on the plane to Cairo and there was concern about weight because the plane was already overloaded. Edgar was asked if he knew anything about gunnery and he was able to say he had been the wireless operator/gunner on an armoured car with the 11th Hussars. That's wonderful they said, so we can dispense with one of the RAF gunners and you can now become wireless / operator gunner for the trip.

Their next stop was Cairo where they landed on the Nile. They stayed for a day before taking off again in the Sunderland for Athens, or Piraeus to be exact. There, Colonel Casson who was Major-General Michael Gambier-Parry's deputy met him. He took him to the Grande Bretagne Hotel in Athens, where the Military Mission was located and up to a large room. He said it was to be his workroom but it also had a bed and furniture in it.

Edgar went out on the hotel roof and he could see that it was ideal for wireless communication. He unpacked the equipment in his room and set up a wireless station with its aerial up on the roof. Within forty-eight hours of arriving at Piraeus, he was able to report that he was in communication with London and Cairo and already exchanging traffic.

Shortly after starting up the station, Edgar mentioned to Colonel Casson that if he were able obtain a suitable vehicle, they had enough equipment to fit out a mobile station. This would enable them to move their base – along the lines of Gambier-Parry's scheme in the UK – and still be in communication with London and Cairo. He was asked what kind of vehicle he had in mind. He replied, although it sounded impossible there in Athens, that at Whaddon they had chosen Packard saloons as being best for the purpose. Lo and behold, a Packard arrived next day and was put at his disposal.

The Grand Bretagne Hotel in Athens one of the most prestigious hotels in Europe was used as the HQ of the British Military Mission. Edgar erected his aerial on its roof and the view is just as he would have seen it in 1940, with the Acropolis in the distance.

A National HRO wireless receiver from the US and a MkIII transmitter made at Whaddon. These are the sets as used by Edgar in Athens – both in his bedroom/wireless station – and in the Packard motorcar.

Edgar duly converted it – just as they had done back at Whaddon and installed the wireless gear. Then he drove Major-General Michael Gambier-Parry and Colonel Casson a fair distance out of Athens where they were soon in communication with both London and Cairo from the Packard. After that Edgar was able to take either of them out of the city and still keep the Mission in touch.

So life went on. He went to the Embassy, introduced himself to the Head of Chancery, the Passport Control Officer and also the two 'Main line' operators who were working to London (Whaddon Hall) and Cairo. They were 'Curly' Meadows and 'Dinger' Bell. They complained to him that their station was either badly sited, or something else was wrong but they had great difficulty in getting through to London and found it almost impossible to communicate with Cairo.

However, Edgar had found it quite easy from his newly constructed station at the Hotel Grande Bretagne so he accepted their request to help them out. He then passed a considerable amount of their traffic to Cairo, a lesser amount to London, and so eased their burden.

Edgar had been only a few days in Athens, when he walked down to Omonia Square in search of somewhere to eat. A Greek civilian, who spoke very good English approached him. He asked if he were an English soldier and he naturally replied, yes!

He told Edgar there was a very good restaurant nearby and asked if he were aware there was now only one meat-day a week in Greece and it happened this was that very day. So Edgar went inside the restaurant with him and they enjoyed a really lovely meal.

He had a 'gorgeous steak with all the trimmings'. Towards the end of the meal, the Greek civilian asked if he spoke any Greek, to which he had to reply, no. He then told Edgar to remember the words 'logariasmo parakalo'. He kept on saying this until Edgar could repeat it word perfect. Then he told him to repeat it when the waiter came to the table, whilst he went off to the toilets. He was away a long time, so when the waiter eventually came to their table, Edgar said 'logariasmo parakalo'. He promptly produced the bill, which Edgar had to pay and he never saw his civilian 'friend' again. However, he certainly learnt how to ask for a bill in Greek – and he would never forget 'logariasmo parakalo'.

So the war lingered on, with the Greeks more than holding their own against the Italians. Then came the day that the Germans decided they would occupy Greece and secure their southern flank. It was expected that they would come through Yugoslavia and the Yugoslavs would put up such resistance it would enable the British – along with the Greeks – to hold a line further south. In the event, nothing of the sort happened, the Germans attacked largely through Bulgaria.

Before they became aware that the Germans had actually entered Greece, Edgar took the Packard mobile station up to Yannina again, having visited the town several times with Michael Gambier-Parry as well as Colonel Casson. The town housed the main British Army base in Greece built by the Royal Army Service Corps and Edgar said it was very extensive and impressive.

His Packard was effectively a Special Liaison Unit or SLU able to pass high grade SIGINT from Cairo and London to the field Commanders. These, and most other intelligence messages they handled, arose in Hut 3 at Bletchley Park. They were sent by teleprinter to the SCU wireless station at Windy Ridge in Whaddon Village, then onwards to Cairo, as well as to Commanders in Greece – via the three operators, Edgar Harrison in the Packard mobile unit, 'Curly' Meadows and 'Dinger' Bell in the 'Main Line' station at the Embassy in Athens.

Traffic increased significantly in early 1941 as the numbers of our forces increased rapidly with troops from Britain, Australia and New Zealand.

In April they were at the base in Yannina when messages of the highest priority started to arrive. Colonel Casson took the deciphered text to a number of senior officers. Shortly afterwards Casson whispered to Edgar that the Germans had attacked through Yugoslavia and that 'the situation is very serious'.

Casson added he had orders to go back to Athens right away and that Edgar should wait for instructions. Shortly afterwards the Greek Army, who had fought so valiantly against the Italians, were overwhelmed as the Germans joined in. It was no contest and on 21st of April 1941 Greece surrendered.

Edgar waited and waited but received no instructions from Casson who had evidently decided to evacuate himself from Greece. As everyone else was leaving the area, Edgar decided he would make his own way back in the Packard to Athens via Larisa. He first loaded up with food and petrol from the army base in Yannina. This was a terrible journey, much worse even than his journey from Brussels to Dunkirk during the Blitzkrieg. He was on his own driving the Packard and bombed and strafed all the way. The Allied air forces already had been utterly destroyed. However, Edgar later said that those who complained about the absence of our Air Force were very much in the wrong. The RAF had suffered appalling casualties but they fought on to the bitter end.

Eventually Edgar arrived in Athens, to find it utterly deserted with no one to be seen and no authority to report to. He then discovered it had been declared an open city. Going to his wireless station in the Grande Bretagne Hotel, he found he could not contact Cairo but was quickly in touch with London and they immediately tried to offer him traffic 'of the highest possible priority'.

Then he did something he would never dream of doing in a normal situation. They had a low grade cypher facility so he encyphered a telegram for Whaddon. He told them he was on his own, that there was no one left in the Mission offices or the Embassy, so he was therefore destroying all his equipment and going to make his way south as best he could. He pointed out that, considering the circumstances, he could not accept the high level SIGINT they were offering. His final words to London were 'destroying cyphers and equipment, goodbye'.

He drove the Packard into the courtyard of the British Embassy, complete with its wireless sets. He destroyed all the wireless equipment but left the car there. He then caught a train going to Corinth that was packed with troops and civilians. It was not molested as far as he knew.

They disembarked from the train at Corinth where there was a great deal of troop movement and were mercilessly bombed and strafed from the air. The attacks continued as they moved away from the station. As Edgar was then ostensibly a sergeant (albeit in MI6 Section VIII and no longer paid by the Army), he collected round him

a number of stragglers from various corps. These had, in one-way or another, been parted from their Regiments and there were no officers to take charge.

With his earlier 'F' Company training, he knew the utmost importance of discipline. Having brought them together, he told them the motto of 'F' Company was 'Stick together and muck in'. It was by adhering to this motto and with the tight discipline he imposed, they arrived together at Argos – in relatively good order after a march of some thirty miles constantly harried by air attacks. Perhaps one should add that by this time Edgar had been a trained soldier for over ten years – probably longer than most of the other troops trying to find their way to safety.

In Argos he found an officer who appeared to be in control and he asked him what they should do. He told Edgar to follow the line of the railway that would take him to the port at Nafplion where he had been told there was a ship. He said he might be able to get on board and be evacuated. So Edgar took his motley crew along with him to march the nine miles to the harbour at Nafplion. Eventually they left the railway line, went across a few fields of corn, broad beans and the like – then over a hill. There, in the sea below was a ship – a most wonderful sight.

Walking purposefully towards the ship, a shot suddenly came over his head and an 'Anzac' voice shouted out, 'the first Pommie bastard that sets foot on this gangway gets it. Bugger off'. They did just that – quite smartly.

As they were leaving, a number of German fighter-bombers came over, and they relentlessly attacked the ship and Edgar's party. They suffered many casualties including Edgar who was wounded by shrapnel in his side. The piece of shrapnel was removed with a pair of pliers by a medical officer of the RAMC (Royal Army Medical Corps). There were dead and wounded all around them. Together with the medical staff, they treated the wounded as best they could, but it was sad having to bury their own dead. These had to be in shallow graves, partly because of the nature of the land, but mainly due to the constant air attacks taking place. They marked the graves as well as possible – under the difficult circumstances.

Edgar assembled what was left of his party and headed back to the railway line. They passed through a field of broad beans and he told the little party to pick the beans, as they had nothing else to eat. This provided them with some kind of sustenance as they made their way back the nine miles to Argos.

By now the town was very crowded, and the officer in charge was in the process of commandeering a train to take them south to Kalamata. Edgar mentioned that he had some knowledge of locomotives and he had a very good knowledge of railway signalling. When the train was all set up, he 'offered' the train on the signalling system and it was accepted. It was single line so he took the 'staff' (a 'key' enabling a train to travel on a single line that is then handed to trains going in the other direction), and so off they went.

This process was repeated until they eventually arrived at Kalamata on 26th April. The city was in absolute turmoil. The Germans had travelled at an unexpectedly high speed down the west coast and had already infiltrated into parts of Kalamata. The Allies had very successfully repelled the first attack, then the Germans arrived in greater numbers and they captured the town.

British, New Zealand and Australian troops, in the olive groves and harbour buildings, were ordered to fix bayonets. They counter-attacked with a bayonet charge and a great battle ensued. During the fierce fighting that

A Greek train similar to the one used to take Allied troops from Port Argos down to Kalamata, with Edgar travelling in the driver's cab to handle the 'Staffs' on the single line track.

followed, Sergeant Hinton, a New Zealand soldier, fought so bravely and effectively that he was subsequently awarded the Victoria Cross. However, in the end the Germans controlled virtually all the town and the Allies were pressed back into the port and beach area, then into large olive groves on the outskirts of the city. Gradually, the crowd of Allied troops spread amongst the olive groves grew into thousands.

At 10pm an order came for them to march back to the port area to be evacuated by the Royal Navy. They were so cheered by this news and tired as they all were, they could have run to the docks. Progress to the port however was very slow – only one destroyer at a time could get in – and embarkation was correspondingly delayed. At last, their destroyer appeared. They inched forward and just when Edgar thought their turn had come to go aboard, a voice said, 'The ship is completely full, sorry, we have to go now – we will pick you up tomorrow.' And off she went. The time was about 3.50am. So it was back to their olive grove to snatch what sleep they could for the rest of the night.

Just before dawn gunfire and enemy aircraft awoke them. They scrambled for as much cover as possible and Edgar said the olive groves did provide a deal of comfort to them, as they tried to get something in the form of breakfast.

The enemy planes were now coming over in far greater numbers and were dropping what they presumed were mines into the harbour and around the port area generally. Also, the enemy infiltrating force had been reinforced and the battle grew in intensity. Reports filtered back of a success on the part of Allied troops – it said they had recaptured the railway station and a number of wounded were brought into the olive groves. The olive groves extended for a distance of at least three miles out from the port area.

As darkness fell and the enemy planes departed, they began to form up for their evacuation when Brigadier Parrington addressed as many as could hear what he had to say. He told them their position was perilous in the extreme. He had no form of communications at all; they had to be patient and see what the hours ahead would bring.

At about 9pm a light came from the anchorage area of the port. It was, they were to learn HMS Hero, one of the five destroyers sent to pick them up. Suddenly, Brigadier Parrington shouted out, 'Is there a signaller about?' Edgar went to his side and the Brigadier said they must get in touch with those ships otherwise they would carry on sailing into the harbour and be blown up by the mines laid during the day.

A torch was found for Edgar, and he blessed forever afterwards his apprenticeship in 'F' company. There, they were taught 'How to establish communication with an unknown station.' He sent out his message in Morse 'AA. AA. AA'. He kept this up until a single light from one of the ships focused on him. He immediately signalled 'STOP. STOP. STOP – DO NOT ENTER THE HARBOUR – IT HAS BEEN MINED.' This was acknowledged. 'Who are you?' came the next signal from what turned out to be HMS Hero.

Brigadier Parrington said tell them, 'We are a very large number of troops, short of ammunition and food. How do you propose to get us off?' Hero replied, 'Every possible boat will be sent to take off as many as we can.'

Edgar then moved down the beach to where there was a small jetty and signalled this was to be the picking up point. He continued communicating with Hero until the first boats

arrived, one of which contained a Royal Navy signaller. His task was done and he felt quite proud that under fire, as it were, he had saved the ships from possible destruction.

Embarkation, albeit ever so slowly, continued until between 3 and 4am when the ship signalled, 'Sorry, we have to leave now'. To which the Brigadier replied, 'Thank you, we now have no option but to surrender'. The last message from Hero was 'Goodbye, God Bless you'. Brigadier Parrington then informed those gathered around that they had to surrender and he sent a German-speaking officer to arrange it.

A drawing from a Newspaper of the time, showing German gunners engaging Allied troops near the water front at Kalamata.

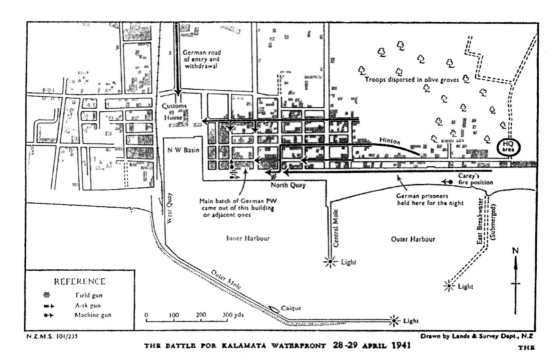

A map of Kalamata water front by the New Zealand Army archives showing where Sergeant Jack Hinton won his VC – refusing to surrender. It also shows the 'troops dispersed in olive trees' that included Edgar all with fixed bayonets.

As far as Edgar was concerned, he decided he was not going to surrender. He thought that anyone aware of his work in Greece with the SIS staff in the Embassy might talk and his life would probably be worth precious little. So off he went.

He had a fairly large sum of drachmas with him, so he spent time in the many caves on the seashore gradually getting further from Kalamata and working out what he should do. His best chance was to collect as much food as possible, acquire a boat, and set out in the hope of being picked up. It was not easy getting food. The Greeks were suspicious but eventually he had sufficient food and water. In order not to disclose his intention, he always immediately walked inland from where he had obtained food or water, before later returning to the coast.

Edgar later learned that at least one other from Kalamata also decided he would not surrender. He had left the town with the intention of finding a boat and paid a Greek to obtain one for him and a few pals who thought likewise. Instead of bringing news of a boat, the Greek returned with a party of German soldiers, and they were taken prisoner. However, they did not congratulate or reward the Greek but shot him there and then – probably on the basis they would never be able to trust him!

Meanwhile Edgar had set off alone along the shoreline, all the time getting further and further away from the chaos at Kalamata. Eventually, he found a boat, conveniently up on the beach, and complete with oars. He got in and rowed away from the shore as quickly as he could. He was not sure how long he spent alone in the rowboat at sea living on the remains of his food and water but it was certainly overnight and into the next day. However, he suddenly spotted a ship on the horizon. He started to wave and surely it was his lucky day, because somebody on a ship spotted this tiny speck in the far distance.

They decided to have a closer look and HMS Kandahar drew alongside Edgar's tiny craft and he was hauled aboard to safety. It truly was a very fortunate day for him, adrift alone in a tiny craft, in the Mediterranean – increasingly dominated by German aircraft.

The captain of the ship came down and said – and Edgar remembered his words quite clearly – 'What in heaven's name were you doing out at sea like that? Have you any knowledge of seamanship?' Edgar replied, 'Not a bit Sir, but I knew the Navy would pick me up.' The captain added, 'I wish I had your bloody faith.'

They warmly welcomed Edgar aboard, fed him and took him on to Crete. He had survived his third retreat.

Edgar refused to surrender and was picked up at sea by HMS Kandahar shown here and taken to Crete. Sadly, the Kandahar was sunk off Tripoli later that year.

Chapter 11

CRETE – OPERATION MERCURY
AND THE FOURTH RETREAT

After being transported to Crete in HMS Kandahar, he thanked its Captain and set about tracing the staff from the Embassy in Athens – who had been evacuated to the island earlier. Finally, he found them in the Consulate and reported in. They then reported his safe arrival to both Cairo and London. Amongst the staff he found there were two SCU men already working on Crete – 'Dinger' Bell and 'Curly' Meadows. These were the operators who had previously been working the 'Main Line' station in the British Embassy in Athens – handling both Embassy and 'Ultra' traffic. They were in a building where ISLD had set up its base on the island. Edgar took his turn with them on watch duty in the wireless room, whilst everyone waited for the anticipated reinforcements to arrive from Egypt.

The initials 'ISLD' stood for Inter Services Liaison Department. This was a pseudonym for SIS used everywhere during World War II, outside of the UK. The impromptu station was handling 'Top Secret' traffic. This was Enigma based intelligence (later to be described as Ultra), from GC&CS at Bletchley Park sent out, via the Section VIII station at 'Windy Ridge' in Whaddon village.

This traffic received by the ISLD wireless team, had been in the form of the 'OL' or 'Orange Leopard' series of signals sent to Cairo with three digits. Later, as the threat to Crete developed, an OL '2000' signal with the prefix '2' indicated to Cairo those messages that had also been sent to Crete direct. Those with the prefix '5' (OL '5000') series were directed to Malta in the same way. Messages to Crete were pre-fixed 'For the attention of General Freyberg'.

The Commander-in-Chief of the Middle East was General Wavell who had recently won a brilliant campaign against the Italians and taken Libya from them. The General appointed to command in Crete (Creforce) was General Freyberg, a New Zealand VC from World War I and greatly favoured by Churchill.

By the time the battle got under way, it appears that the ISLD wireless station was re-located nearer the 'Creforce' GHQ, which was based in a quarry close to Halepa, a village near the town of Canea. The SLU officer responsible for handling Ultra was Captain Mike Sandover, an Intelligence Officer from the Australian Army. His intelligence team, including an army wireless interception facility, was working nearby in a cave in part of the quarry.

In accordance with the very strict SLU instructions, the team of Bell, Harrison and Meadows would have been housed apart from them, and kept busy with Ultra traffic. The number of OL signals logged gives some indication of the volume from that quarter alone. Bear in mind, they were also receiving lower grade SIGINT as well from Cairo and London – so Bell and Meadows must have been pleased to have Edgar Harrison join the team and share the rapidly growing work load.

Major-General Freyberg VC Commander of the Allied troops at the time of the German attack on Crete – May 20th 1941.

Suddenly, in the early morning of May 20th waves of German dive-bombers and fighter aircraft attacked the Maleme, Canea, and Suda Bay areas with the heaviest bombing they had yet received. Their defences, including crucially their anti-aircraft guns, were quickly put out of action.

General Kurt Student of the Luftwaffe and Commander of the German paratrooper attack on Crete, code-named Merkur (Mercury).

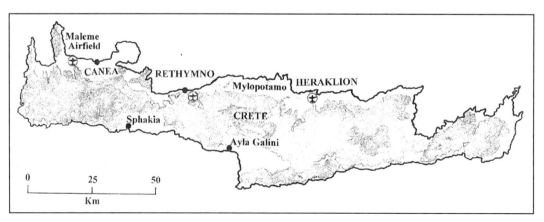

This was the start of the German invasion of Crete that they had given the code-name of 'Merkur' – Mercury! It was under the overall command of General Kurt Student, one of the most able German Generals and closely associated with the Blitzkrieg attacks in Western Europe. He was known to be a strong believer in the decisive role that parachute troops could play in warfare.

The sky over Crete during the attack – one Ju57 has been hit and is crashing.

German paratroops on the ground engaging Allied forces.

Paratroopers landing on Crete in Operation 'Mercury'.

Around 08.00, the first gliders landed near the Maleme airfield, and onto the beaches on the northern side of the island. This wave of gliders coincided with the launch of something over 2000 parachutists in the biggest airborne assault ever carried out to that time.

These parachutists were caught in heavy small arms fire from those defending the airfields and the German casualties were very heavy. They included the Commander of the German 7th Airborne Division General Wilhelm Suessmann who was killed during his approach to the island and Generalmajor Meindell, commanding the Maleme assault, was critically wounded soon after landing.

The German airborne assault went on relentlessly and a seaborne invasion was attempted on 20th and 22nd of May. This was attacked by ships of the Royal Navy causing heavy losses to the mostly mountain troops on board the freighters and motor-sailers being used. The Navy thus prevented the landing of the much needed reinforcements, artillery, ammunition and supplies for the German attackers. A second German convoy of troops and supplies was recalled, to prevent it suffering a similar fate.

On the night of May 20th / May 21st British and New Zealand troops withdrew from Maleme airfield, unfortunately leaving it open for full use by follow-up aircraft, all bringing reinforcements and supplies. On 22nd May the German 8th Air Corps mounted a savage and sustained attack on the British fleet, which was then forced to leave the Aegean. Gradually, their overwhelming airpower led them to quickly control all the air space and the sea, north of Crete.

After a few days of sustained bombing and strafing and the continued build up of German troops, it was decided to remove the ISLD unit and its wireless operators

General Freyberg during the battle.

Allied troops waiting to go into action.

from the island. Quite apart from anything else, it was absolutely vital that they be protected from possible capture. Obviously their knowledge of the operational side of the Ultra traffic was a vital secret. They destroyed their wireless equipment, burnt the codebooks and all traces of the Ultra operation. There followed a difficult journey under air attack and then, in the last days of May and just before the final surrender of the island, the three ISLD operators, Edgar Harrison, 'Dinger' Bell and 'Curly' Meadows, were embarked on a Naval vessel and taken to Alexandria.

There, Edgar was greeted by Colonel Casson, who was absolutely delighted to see him. He said that he was so sorry to have left Edgar on his own at Yannina but when he got back to Athens, most of the Mission were just whisked straight onto a flying boat at Piraeus and off to Cairo. He said he had no time to alert Edgar about anything and added – 'You must know how pleased I am to see you!'

Back in Egypt, Edgar realised he had been forced to retreat from Norway, Dunkirk, Greece and now Crete, making four retreats in the space of around twelve months.

The battle for Crete waged on for a few days, with British Commonwealth and detachments of Cretan and Greek troops – made the Germans fight for every inch of land. However, German air power and the continued flow of fresh troops from Greece led inevitably to the decision to evacuate the island beginning on June 1st. The Royal Navy were able to embark about 14,500 men over a period of four nights but they sustained heavy losses and some 12,000 Allied troops were left behind.

It is worth noting in this very brief summary of the battle for Crete – which proved so costly to the Germans – they never again attempted the large-scale use of paratroops. Some 23,000 of their finest troops had been deployed for Operation Mercury and over 7,000 were killed or wounded. The German paratroops withdrawn after the battle, mostly perished later in Russia – highly trained soldiers of the highest calibre – simply wasted in the misery and horror of that front.

There are a number of reasons for Hitler attacking Yugoslavia, then Greece and Crete. Undoubtedly he was concerned about the poor performance of the

Left behind in Crete: British troops taken prisoner by German Paratroopers. It was essential that Edgar Harrison and his colleagues from Section VIII did not share their fate.

Italians fighting the Greeks in Albania and felt it necessary to secure his southern flank, before his attack on Russia.

Overall, the campaign in Greece and the battle for Crete lasted some five weeks and was responsible for Hitler's original launch date for Operation Barbarossa being delayed some six weeks. The result of that delay was that he was not able to capture Moscow and defeat the bulk of the Red Army, before the terrible Russian winter set in. In a real way, the desperate fight put up by the Greeks and their Allies, the British, Australian and New Zealand forces, became the source of the failure of the German campaign in Russia.

Troops landing at Alexandria after being evacuated from Crete.

A vigorous resistance campaign was instituted almost immediately after the fall of the island and remained active until 1945. This campaign necessitated an Axis garrison of some 50,000 personnel at its peak – troops who could have been used to great effect in other theatres.

Winston Churchill later gave a speech in which he made this famous statement: "Hence we shall not say that Greeks fight like heroes, but that heroes fight like Greeks."

(Appendix 5 deals with the situation in Greece and Crete).

Chapter 12

RECUPERATION AND JOINING ISLD IN CAIRO

Now safely in Egypt, Edgar had a couple of days rest in Alexandria. Later Colonel Casson gave him money to travel by train to the ISLD headquarters at Abassia just outside Cairo.

There he found that an ISLD unit had been formed in Cairo in 1940 by Captain Bawlby of the Royal Navy and consisted of Arab, Greek, Italian, and Yugoslav sections. Also under its control was the Section VIII 'Main Line' wireless station handling ISLD wireless traffic since all its covert communications had been made the responsibility of Richard Gambier-Parry's SCU (Special Communication Units).

Immediately on arrival Edgar was taken to hospital as his wound sustained at Nafplio in Greece needed further treatment and more importantly, they discovered there were tiny particles of shrapnel in one eye. However, immediately on reaching the hospital he suddenly collapsed with a mysterious illness – thought to be Sand Fly fever.

He woke up two days later and found himself in the military hospital at Gazira. He later heard a voice saying 'Edgar, Edgar'. He looked up and there was his brother Wallace – a sergeant in the Royal Corps of Signals – at his bedside. Wallace said he had been

Troops dug-in at Tobruk. This coastal town remained a thorn in the side of Rommel for many months after he crossed the border into Egypt. Wallace Harrison was wounded here whilst a wireless operator with 7th Armoured Division Signals.

searching for Edgar and found him by checking the hospital lists. He had been with the 7th Armoured Division and wounded outside Tobruk. He was now fully recovered having been earlier brought back to Cairo for treatment and recuperation.

Edgar had an operation on his eye in a specialist unit and with the wound in his side healing, he was sent for a short period of convalescence at Skouriotissa in northern Cyprus. On his return, now declared fit for service, he went to the ISLD offices in Cairo to make himself known. There he found that his friend Charles Emary, by now a Captain, was in charge of its wireless station.

A street in Heliopolis, a quarter in Cairo containing ISLD offices and where some of its staff were billeted.

He thought Emary was finding it too much of a burden and it came as little surprise when he was later recalled home. He was replaced by Wing-Commander Jock Adamson RAF who had been in the Royal Flying Corps in World War I. Edgar instantly took a great liking to the man and they got on very well. All these men, Army and RAF were members of Richard Gambier-Parry's Special Communication Unit.

Edgar in civilian clothes whilst living and working in Cairo.

He was able to make arrangements for Wallace to be transferred into Section VIII where he became a member of its engineering team. Wallace was an excellent wireless engineer, as distinct from himself, whom he always considered to be primarily a wireless operator. Like all members of Section VIII – both kept their uniforms and nominal rank but were paid by MI6 and free to wear civilian clothes. For much of this time Edgar, in line with others in ISLD, did indeed wear civilian clothes especially around the wireless stations at Abassia and Riverside.

Edgar carried out various tasks at the station and it was a quite enjoyable period. Secret agents were being trained inside the base in the use of Morse and the Whaddon-made agents' wireless sets and as he recovered Edgar took an increasing share in the training. Richard Gambier-Parry provided three main communication links to and from Cairo.

First was 'Main Line' at Abassia and that handled covert and some Embassy traffic to

A mobile SLU unit working SIGINT and Ultra traffic. Edgar is second left back row. To his left is Wing Commander 'Jock' Adamson, then the Head of Section VIII in the Middle East. Kneeling bottom right is Norman 'Plug' Walton. He had gone out with several Packards forming the original 'A' Detachment from Whaddon to handle Ultra right into our Military Commanders in the field.

Baghdad, Basra, Istanbul, Jerusalem, Malta – and of course to London and Bletchley Park – via the 'Main Line' wireless station in the grounds of Whaddon Hall. Secondly, an agents' station working to our agents in North Africa, Asia Minor, Crete, Greece, Italy and Yugoslavia.

The agent's station was quite separate from Main Line although top-rank operators like Edgar would help out at both of them in times of exceptional traffic. Some of the other operators at that high level in Cairo at the time, included George Heigho who Edgar regarded as the fastest telegraphist he had ever known and had come from Reuters and Chris Lovell who came from Cable and Wireless in Aden.

The third element was the SCU/SLUs of 'A Detachment'. In early 1941 Gambier-Parry had sent the detachment to North Africa under the command of Lt. Col. Kenneth McFarlane – originally of the Royal Artillery – but now a long serving and important member of MI6. The 'A Detachment' consisted of a number of Packard saloon motorcars fitted out at Whaddon Hall as mobile wireless stations. Their equipment included a MkIII transmitter made in Whaddon's workshops and either an HRO or a Hallicrafters wireless receiver – both of these having been made in the US.

The role of 'A Detachment' was to park their wireless and cypher vehicles right alongside the Army (or Air Command) HQ in the field. There it passed on top-secret 'Signals Intelligence' (SIGINT) to the Army Commanders, from Bletchley Park. Later some of this traffic would be known as 'Ultra' but only when it was of the highest level.

This Signals Intelligence went to them, via Gambier-Parry's 'Special Operations Group' in the wireless station at 'Windy Ridge' at Whaddon, to the Main Line station in Cairo, then relayed onwards to these mobile stations. Group Captain Fred Winterbotham had called them 'Special Liaison Units'. 'A Detachment' was the first unit of its kind sent abroad apart from the two improvised cars that had been sent out in early 1940 to the BEF in France.

'A Detachment' was the forerunner of the mobile SCU/SLUs that played such a great part in the Allied 'Torch' invasion of western north Africa under General Eisenhower. Later they played a major role in providing 'Ultra' messages from Bletchley Park to our commanders after D-Day – thus substantially assisting the overthrow of the enemy forces in France and Germany.

Chapter 13

YUGOSLAVIA AND THE FIFTH RETREAT

After being at ISLD HQ in Cairo for a short time, Edgar was summoned to the Yugoslav Section at ISLD. He was told he had to go to Yugoslavia and was asked if he had any objection to parachute jumping? He agreed to go to Kanka airfield, not far from Cairo where he had training, consisting of three practice jumps from 3000 feet and that was that. Incidentally, he says it was amazing how near the ground appears from 3000 feet – it seemed to be more like 300 feet!

This limited training, that I understand occupied only a few days, compares rather badly with the many weeks later devoted to the entrants to the newly formed Parachute Regiments.

His mission was to take wireless equipment to General Mihailovic in Yugoslavia who was desperate for secure high-level communications. His task was to set up the wireless stations that ISLD had promised to him. Edgar was told this was not to be a journey by sea but meant he had to drop into Yugoslavia by parachute.

He was to be parachuted into Yugoslavia wearing the uniform of a Lieutenant in the Royal Corps of Signals. However, officially he was still a Sergeant in the Royal Corps of Signals although by now a member of MI6 (Section VIII) and NPAF (Not Paid Army Funds). Members of Section VIII could be dressed according to the assignment they were on. In this case, it was felt necessary for an Army (or ISLD) representative who would meet General Mihailovic during his work to be an officer.

2nd/Lieut. Edgar Harrison of Section VIII in 1941.

General Draza Mihailovic was a Serb, educated at the Military Academy who became an officer in World War I and was a Colonel at the outbreak of World War II. After the invasion in 1941, he began offering strong resistance to the Germans and Italians with an army gathered round him, called 'Chetniks'. Throughout 1941 and into early 1943, Mihailovic, with his Chetniks, was the leader on whom British hopes – maybe especially MI6 hopes – rested in Yugoslavia.

This was before it became obvious that the Communist Partisans, under the leadership of Tito, were making the greatest impact on the occupying forces. Although the British knew of Tito at the time that Edgar was sent into Yugoslavia, they were currently pinning their hopes of defeating the Germans on the Chetnik forces under Mihailovic.

General 'Draza' Mihailovic leader of the Chetnik forces in Yugoslavia.

Opposite: General Josip Broz Tito leader of the Yugoslav Partisans.

The Chetniks were a Serbian nationalist and royalist organisation, with origins going back to the Serbian opposition to the Ottoman rule in World War I. In World War II, they rallied round the title of 'The Yugoslav Royal Army in the Fatherland' – founded in May 1941.

They had a burning hatred of the Communist Partisans under Tito and whilst both men fought the Germans and the Italians they also fought one another. Tito seemed determined to establish a Communist controlled greater Yugoslavia and Mihailovic wanted one dominated by Serbia. The same vicious inter-racial, inter-religious wars that now ensued had erupted from time to time – over many years. This then, was the background to the vicious war being conducted across Yugoslavia as Edgar was parachuted in.

His wireless and other equipment was collected and somehow they managed to find him a space on a plane that was taking SOE personnel into Yugoslavia. SOE – 'Special Operations Executive' – were quite separate from SIS and concerned with an active and aggressive role to the occupation forces of a country. It was formed soon after Dunkirk, out of an idea from Winston Churchill to ensure continued harassment of the occupying forces and to lay the ground for the Allies to return.

By this time, parties of SOE personnel were beginning to be sent to Yugoslavia to assess which of the two factions to support, bearing in mind it was the eventual aim of the Allies to strike back into Europe, via Yugoslavia.

They took off in the evening and after a few hours flying they received recognition signals from the ground. They dropped their equipment first and then all the SOE personnel on board left the aircraft, followed by the lone figure of Edgar.

The reception party was there and thankfully all was in order. Everyone's equipment was collected and the two Yugoslavs who were assigned to Edgar, quickly sorted out his equipment from that of the SOE. He said goodbye and good luck to his SOE companions who left immediately.

General Mihailovic with his staff officers.

The Yugoslavs had pack animals with them and Edgar's group loaded his equipment onto them, and he reckoned that within an hour they had left the point where they had landed. There was no pause as they travelled through the darkness and daybreak found them on the outskirts of a scattered community. The Yugoslavs now indicated that they must exercise great caution, make sure their weapons were loaded and ready to fire.

Edgar's first resting place for the day was in an outbuilding, quite comfortable and what food they had, principally a kind of thick soup was acceptable and nourishing. With each meal, copious quantities of wine were available. However, he stuck almost exclusively to water.

Dusk found them on the trail again. This time they made much better progress and his colleagues appeared to be happier. It was obvious the further they were away from the landing point, the safer they felt. By dawn, they found themselves near a very large village and Edgar thought he once heard the sound of a car. Anyway, there were lots of people about, his companions were greeted like long-lost brothers and he was kissed over and over again. It was apparent this village wholeheartedly supported the Chetnik cause and he was not unhappy to learn he would be staying there a while.

He felt the time had now come to unpack and assemble the wireless equipment. He sought advice as to how and where this might be carried out. There was no problem. A very large basement was found for him, all wired up, but sadly without

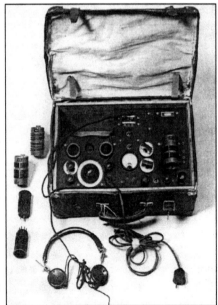

A MkV suitcase transceiver made at Whaddon Hall.

power. This was because there was no fuel for the local generator. Edgar was not unduly perturbed at the lack of a main supply as his 'Tiny Tim' generator-cum-battery charger could provide all the power he needed to test the gear.

Over the next 24 hours he completed the assembly and testing and was very happy to find it all in good working order. On the day following his drop one of the locals arrived and gave him a 'sit-up-and-beg' bicycle, indicating that it was for Edgar's sole use in an area where the only other form of transport was one's own two feet.

A MkIII transmitter, another product from Section VIII workshops at Whaddon Hall. It is likely that Edgar would have used this himself and doubtful if he were to have left such a set behind.

We are fortunate that Edgar describes the suitcase sets he took with him, as being 21 x 12 x 8 inches and that was probably the Whaddon-made MkV transceiver. In any case, it was probably too early for the smaller MkVII set he used on his later journeys with Winston Churchill and elsewhere. That model was only just going into limited production in 1942.

Having made the equipment secure, Edgar set off on his bike with his two Yugoslav companions, to be introduced to most of the Chetnik hierarchy. They must have travelled at least 15 miles before being challenged by numerous guards who escorted them to General Mihailovic's Chief of Staff. Edgar was then introduced to the General and explained what he was sent to do for them.

Thankfully, the General and most of his immediate subordinates spoke good English, so it took Edgar little time to explain how he considered his wireless gear could be best used to their advantage. There was no disagreement and following a decent meal, transport was arranged to fetch all his equipment to their headquarters.

When it arrived, he then discovered one of the most difficult parts of his task, that of dealing with the Chetniks' own communication staff. He started by showing them the equipment and how he thought it could best be used.

Having listened, the Chetnik operators and wireless engineers then told him to hand over all his equipment and leave them to get on with it. Edgar said as they could not possibly have any knowledge of this equipment (made at Whaddon Hall), they would at least need guidance. His strict instructions were to install wireless to enable Mihailovic to contact Cairo and London also for internal communications.

Although they now backed down a little, he found them an arrogant and uncooperative group who decided they knew best. Having set up the first station, he made contact with both Cairo and London (Whaddon) and it was an excellent link. Edgar then showed them how to get the best out of the MkIII transmitter and most importantly to care for its crystals since without them no communication was possible.

He travelled with Mihailovic to a number of places. They set up outstations and were almost continuously on the move whilst a very savage kind of war raged

A group of Chetnik fighters alongside German soldiers.

around them. At first, Edgar could not understand what the fighting was about, until it dawned on him that at times they were not fighting the Italians and the Germans – instead they were fighting Croats and Slovenes who had been armed by the Germans.

It was a very nasty situation. The out-stations Edgar had been ordered to set up were between twenty and sixty miles from Headquarters that involved travel through terrain occupied partly by Croatians and Slovenes. He became closely involved in many brutal engagements with much bloodshed. Indeed so closely that he became personally caught up in the fighting. Some of his companions were killed and others wounded alongside him. It was civil war at its worst.

German Major-General Friedrich Stahl with a Ustasi officer and a Chetnik commander, Rade Radic in central Bosnia.

Edgar said it was a terrible state of affairs when trust could not be placed in those around them, with friend and foe almost indistinguishable. It was the constant fear of betrayal and the deceit that concerned him most. There was such hatred and slaughter with no quarter asked and none given. He later said that it was the worst fighting he witnessed throughout the whole of World War II.

The General congratulated him on his success in placing out-stations under such extremely hazardous conditions. He said Edgar's work under fire would not go unrecorded or unrewarded and Mihailovic reported so to Cairo. Edgar was delighted beyond measure, when word came through that he should leave the country and return to Cairo. He was given a rendezvous point on the coast where he was to be picked up by a submarine and then taken back to Alexandria.

After many an adventure on the way with considerable and bloody fighting, Edgar found himself at the allotted beach rendezvous point. After the correct signals were exchanged, a rubber dingy approached and he was taken out to the safety of HMS Perseus a submarine of the Royal Navy. All he remembered of his submarine journey back to Alexandria was the dreadful smell. For this journey he was a naval officer but later reverted to civilian clothes in Cairo.

HM Submarine Perseus sent to take Edgar off from the Yugoslavian mainland. It was lost only a short while after his rescue – in the Ionian Sea.

Edgar wondered how submariners lived in such conditions but assumed they simply became used to it in time. He thought it was truly awful and that submariners – whatever their pay – earned every single penny. [Tragically, HMS Perseus was lost later that year on 6th December 1941 – in the Ionian Sea off the coast of Kefalonia – with the loss of fifty-nine officers and men].

However, Edgar was made welcome in the wardroom at Alexandria (Raseltin, where the Royal Navy had their headquarters). He later took a train back to Cairo and this was still in 1941. His journey back from the hell of Yugoslavia was his fifth retreat.

(Appendix 6 briefly describes the main warring factions in Yugoslavia and Appendix 7 explains the ease with which appointments were made in MI6 – Section VIII.)

Chapter 14

RUSSIA AND EDGAR'S SIXTH RETREAT

Shortly after returning from Yugoslavia, Edgar was asked to attend at the Embassy in Cairo. There, the Ambassador – Lord Killearn – whom Edgar had known as Sir Miles Locker Lampson in Peking in 1933, when he was the Minister at the Legation there – invited him to be a member of a small Mission to Southern Russia.

It was explained to him that the Russians had sent a 'shopping list' to the Allies and whilst the bulk of supplies would still be sent to Russia via Murmansk and Archangel, it was considered a good idea to open up another route into Russia via the Arabian Gulf ports and Iran. After unloading the supplies at Iranian ports, two routes were available. One by rail Ahwaz–Teheran–Tabriz, the other via the Caspian Sea to Baku, and then to the battlefront.

John Bruce Lockhart (son of Robert Bruce Lockhart, the famous Russian scholar who had been involved with Lenin in Russia) and Edgar, left Cairo in late October. They then met up with the other members of the Mission at Habaniyah. This was a major RAF base in Iraq and for sheer luxury this important airport took some beating. The other nine members of the Mission were mostly seconded from the Indian Army. Sadly, Edgar did not remember the names of everyone in this small Mission. Head of the Mission was a Colonel R. E. ('George') Way,

A trainload of tanks on the way to Russia. It was quite common to see such loads in the UK marked 'Tanks for Russia' as part of the PR support for the Soviet war effort – pending the opening of the Second Front.

RA (Royal Artillery) but significantly he was also Deputy Director of Military Intelligence. His second-in-command was a Captain Edwardes. Both Colonel Way and Captain Edwardes spoke fluent Russian.

Edwardes was a particularly interesting chap. Born in Istanbul of a mixed Welsh/Russian parentage he also spoke Turkish and Greek, in addition to flawless Russian. After the war, he became Chairman of British Petroleum. Apart from Way and Edwardes, the Mission contained cypher personnel – a Captain and a sergeant – two clerks, two Russian speaking Indian Army Captains with unspecified duties, and a Captain Dean from the Royal Signals. The latter did not speak Russian, neither did the clerks or cypher officers. Edgar had a slight knowledge of Russian that he had gained in China during the 1930s.

Ostensibly, Edgar's specific brief was to accompany wireless equipment to the immediate rear of the battlefront, to install the equipment into armoured vehicles, and to instruct selected Russians in its use and maintenance. However, the fact is that he accompanied John Bruce Lockhart separately from the main team and joined them at Habaniyah. We know that Bruce Lockhart was also in ISLD (SIS) – so we have two ISLD members *and* the Deputy Director of Military Intelligence in a team – seemingly just about supplies. (See appendix 8)

When Edgar was satisfied that there were sufficient competent Russian instructors, the announced aim was that he could return to Cairo. It sounded easy. He was also to set up a wireless link with Cairo, London, Baghdad and Kuybeshev. It should be noted that the Russian Government, together with all the accredited foreign Embassies, had moved to Kuybeshev from Moscow, in face of the possible occupation of the Russian capital by the Germans.

To go back in time. The Mission left Habaniyah in an old RAF 'Wellesley' aircraft and it flew slowly – following the railway track – to Mosul. The aircraft was so slow that at times they felt the trains were going faster than them.

At Mosul, where they arrived before lunch, a Russian built DC3 Dakota awaited them. After what appeared interminable delays, they set off for Tbilisi, the Georgian capital. They were not, however, destined to reach Tbilisi that day or the next. They had a great deal to learn about Russian bureaucracy.

Their first short flight brought them to Nakichevan, a largish town in a disputed part of Armenia. There they were whisked from the plane to a nondescript hotel and told they had to stay there until the next morning when they would be collected.

So their first taste of Russian hospitality was twelve hours in a third-rate hotel without food. They had no roubles so they could not buy anything to eat. They took off next day and later landed at Erevan the Armenian capital.

After booking into a slightly better hotel than at Nakichevan, they were surprisingly let out into the town for a few hours. A late October day, clear blue skies, pleasantly warm, just the day for a stroll through the town then find a seat in a park and observe Armenian life – twas not to be!

Edgar hadn't gone much more than a couple of hundred yards when two English-speaking Armenians accosted him. Although they knew perfectly well he was a British soldier, they harangued him incessantly about the superiority of the Soviet system. At times, he thought they would physically assault him. There was no question of him getting in a word in either English or Russian. He was there to be indoctrinated. Obviously there was a limit to his endurance so, after about an hour's persecution, he returned to the hotel.

At the hotel he discovered that other Russian-speaking members of the Mission had been similarly accosted; it was apparent the Russians had pre-warned the local Commissars of their names and they had been singled out for the treatment.

They were pleased to leave Erevan the following day and continue their flight. They later landed at the Georgian capital Tbilisi, with hopes of better treatment from the Russians at what they discovered, was to be their headquarters. To a certain extent these hopes were realised when they were settled into the Hotel Tbilisi, the best hotel in Georgia. A whole floor of the hotel was allotted to them and Edgar was pleased to have his own room with bath and toilet – western style. In Erevan and Nakichevan the toilets had been what were known as 'Turkish' or squatting closets.

By noon the next day, Edgar had erected aerials on the hotel roof and was in contact with London, Cairo, Baghdad and Kuybeshev. His first telegram from Cairo was pleasant enough – promotion to Captain in Section VIII – and details of a pay rise for him from Charlie Crocker, the Section VIII paymaster. That evening they all assembled in a private room on the ground floor and were introduced to the Russians with whom they were to do business.

Generally speaking the Russians outranked them. Included in the welcoming committee was their 'Perivochka'. She was to be the official translator for the Mission. The daughter of the physician to the late Tsar, her name was Veroshka Snegiriva. Her English was impeccable and *very* English. During their stay at Tbilisi they made many attempts to talk her over to their way of thinking, but to no avail. She was a totally loyal Communist Party member.

While waiting for news of the stores and equipment for the Russians, they made the fullest use of what spare time came their way. Their first job was to locate the British war cemetery, which they found in an appalling condition on the outskirts of Tbilisi. It may not be generally known that British troops were fighting in Russia up to 1921 and Georgia and Azerbaijan were the two areas where they made their final attempt to overthrow the Red Army. It will be known that the War Graves Commission has the responsibility for looking after the British war cemeteries and it is widely acknowledged that they do a splendid job.

However, after the last British Consul left Tbilisi in (Edgar thought) the early 1930s, Georgia was closed to us. Anyway, they cleared and cleaned up the cemetery as best they could and took note of the names of the dead.

There were many more than they had first thought. Edgar then telegraphed brief details of what they had done to London and Kuybeshev, and from London they received authority to employ a part-time Georgian gardener to look after the cemetery. They found out later that the man they took on had been a Russian Orthodox priest. Edgar wondered what happened to him and the cemetery after they left.

Incidentally, without wishing to appear morbid, he suggests that whenever one is in a foreign country where our armed forces have served, one should take the opportunity to visit the war cemetery. He found such visits very moving indeed.

Next on their list was transport and here they drew a blank. The Russians were willing to let Colonel Way have a car, on request, for specific purposes. For the rest of them, it was a bus twice a week to the local stadium to play football. Otherwise their journeys were on foot or by the local trams. The latter were very cheap and they used them extensively.

A football team at a stadium in Tiblisi consisting of local Georgians and members of the Way Mission whilst waiting to go into the Ukraine. Edgar is sitting bottom left.

Captain Edwardes in his spare time, went to performances by the Georgian Opera Group. He fell in love with the Prima Donna and proposed to her. In her acceptance, she said that she had to be married in red silk or satin. In true Section VIII fashion, the material was obtained – probably from Cairo – and they were married.

Edgar mentioned here the state of the roads they encountered in the Soviet Union. In Nakichevan and Erevan the best one could hope for was the occasional cobbled surface, which was usually monopolised by the trams. Tbilisi could boast a few macadamised roads, the Prospect Rushta Rustevilli (named after Georgia's most famous poet), being a particularly fine thoroughfare. Away from the few macadam roads, it was cobbled or packed earth roads everywhere.

As far as money was concerned, they were given a special rate to purchase roubles; otherwise even the very few things available for sale would have been beyond their purse. Their food and accommodation at the hotel was paid out of public funds, so what money they spent, largely went on drinks in the hotel bar, ice-cream, transport and souvenirs.

Whilst waiting, a fairly typical day for Edgar in Tbilisi went something like this. Up at 06.00 and, after his wash and shave, commenced his wireless contacts. These were usually Baghdad at 07.00, Cairo at 07.30 and Kuybeshev at 08.00. After the Kuybeshev contact he had breakfast, and then contacted London (Whaddon), at 10.00. These times were local, and were three hours ahead of GMT.

The day's briefing with Colonel Way depended on his commitments with the Russians but they usually managed a daily briefing at 12.00 followed by lunch. Whilst in Tbilisi, Edgar's afternoons were largely free as the amount of telegraphic traffic handled was not great. Shortly after their arrival in Tbilisi, Edgar had used his spare receiver to give the Mission news from the BBC. He wired it into a speaker in their briefing room and the reception was usually excellent – with no jamming in those days.

They spent many hours in the briefing room listening to the BBC, either saddened or uplifted as the fortunes of war swung this way and that, whilst they enjoyed Georgian wine and endured Russian beer.

On two occasions, the Georgians went out of their way to offer them diversions of a sort. First, those who could ride were invited to a boar hunt. Edgar went and although some boars were killed, he did not see a live boar himself. This boar hunt took place in a forest some 20 miles north of Tbilisi.

The second invitation, this time to the whole Mission, was to a Collective Farm an hour's drive from their hotel. Despite the protestations of their perivoshka that their visit to the farm was unexpected, it was obviously a well planned visit.

The Elder of the farm welcomed them with a speech in Georgian, courteously delivered and apparently friendly. There followed an extensive tour of the farm during which norms and quotas were frequently mentioned. If one was to believe what was said, quotas had been raised by 100 per cent since the outbreak of war.

They all enjoyed lunch at the farm, one of the best meals they had in the Soviet Union, certainly the best lunch. Home cured hams, home made bread, pickles and other preserves, and lovely salads.

After lunch Edgar asked if he could go for a short walk and during this stroll he saw a series of wonderfully productive pieces of land. He wondered why they hadn't been shown them on their conducted tour and was told by one of the farm workers that these were their own private plots of land. After the farm workers had fulfilled their stint on the Collective, they were allowed to farm whatever they wished on their own plots. Edgar guessed that the private plots were at least 50 per cent more productive than the Collective.

Now, before going on to relate affairs in the Ukraine, Edgar wished to tell of an almost unbelievable encounter he had in Tbilisi – some two weeks after their arrival. The bus had dropped him off at the front of the hotel where they were staying and, as he was about to enter the hotel, three ladies confronted him.

Two he placed in the sixties and the other in her forties, all were dressed in a genteel but shabby way. They were all above average height. One of the older ladies then said, 'Excuse me, but are you one of the English soldiers?' (Edgar was in football gear having returned from playing a match at Tbilisi stadium). He replied, yes, and then asked if she were English. 'Oh no,' the lady replied, 'I am French,' and turning to the other older lady, she said *she* was English.

Eventually Edgar sorted it out. He found he was in the company of 'Miss English' and a 'Miss French'. More about the younger lady later on. He invited them into the hotel for a cup of tea and biscuits, where the others joined them and then they unfolded their amazing tale.

Either in 1899, 1900, or 1901, they weren't exactly sure – but they knew Queen Victoria was on the throne – three ladies in their early twenties, ex-Cheltenham; accepted employment as governesses to the Royal Princes of Georgia. Specifically, they were to bring up the Royal children and instil into them good old British values. It was a full and varied life, lots of travelling throughout Russia and they loved it.

One event, however, did mar their happiness. Not long after they arrived in Tiflis, as it was then called, one of the governesses became pregnant by the elder son of the ruling prince and the younger lady, who was at the hotel entrance, was the child of this pregnancy. The three governesses brought up the girl as one of their 'royal' family and when the girl's mother died during the 1914-18 War, Miss English and Miss French became her parents.

1917 saw the birth of the Russian revolution, but this event did not, at first, make any difference to the lifestyle of the Princes of Georgia and their governesses. It was 1919 before clashes between the Red and White Armies came anywhere near Georgia. By 1921, however, the writing was on the wall for the White Army and Allied troops supporting this Army were withdrawn from Russia. By 1922 Georgia was firmly inside the Soviet borders.

They asked Miss English and Miss French why they did not leave Tiflis with the Allied forces as they could have done. They said, to them it was a matter of loyalty to the children of the now *ex*-royal family. They felt it was their duty to stand by them through thick and thin and this they had done right up to that present day – November 1941.

They then asked the ladies how they had managed, and were managing, for money. This question obviously embarrassed them, it was evident they were hard up and living in near poverty. However, they were nothing if not proud and they told the men they taught English privately. They had a few roubles saved up, but the advent of the war had made life difficult.

They kept saying, it was all right when the Consulate was there; when they wanted money for something special the Consul always gave them an allowance. They asked when the Consul had left and were told the Consulate closed when the Germans invaded Russia.

At this point they decided it was time to take the ladies home and this they did in their 'football' bus after promising to collect them the following day for tea.

Armed with the information given to them by the three ladies, Edgar was authorised to contact London and Kuybeshev by wireless the next day, giving them the fullest particulars they had, and requested authority to make the ex-governesses a monthly allowance. Both replied later in the day to say they had no record of any Miss English or Miss French or the deceased governess.

London, however, authorised the payment of a monthly allowance and their telegram – as did Kuybeshev's – ended by saying the last British Consul left Tiflis in the 1920s and the Consulate had been closed since that time. Very strange!

At the second tea party, they told the governesses of their success in getting them a monthly allowance, which pleased them greatly. They then said they were puzzled about the Consul from whom the ladies had obtained their allowance, as there had been no British Consul in Tiflis for years. Were they *absolutely* sure about the Consul?

Edgar was never to forget the rather patronising look Miss English and Miss French gave them – as they said in unison – 'Of course we didn't go to the British Consulate, we always went to our friend the German Consul' (Frederick von something or other). 'He was our dearest friend and he looked after us right up to the day he had to leave.'

Then they enquired further of London and Kuybeshev. This took them nowhere; no

The dreadful winter conditions found on the Russian front.

authority had ever been given to the German Government to pay monies to Miss French or Miss English. All they could assume was that the German Consul – out of the goodness of his heart – had seen that the ex-governesses were never in real want.

They asked a final question at the second tea party. Were they fluent in Russian and Georgian? 'Oh no,' was the reply, 'we speak only English'. Then they were asked how they managed to buy essentials like food, drink, and kerosene?

'Quite simple really, we have taught them to speak and understand English!'

What a formidable couple, rarely had Edgar felt so proud of his own folk.

They saw them regularly during their stay in Tbilisi, as Tiflis became in 1936. Their final farewell, when they unloaded all their spare roubles, food and clothes on the ladies, was a very tearful affair. It was no good promising to write, as during their whole stay in Russia, not a single personal letter got through to them. The day before they left, the ladies showed them the plots of land they had obtained in the cemetery alongside their deceased friend and members of the 'royals' they had looked after.

Now, they will be at rest in their adopted land. Bless them. Edgar said he would never forget them.

Towards the end of November word came through that a large consignment of stores had arrived at Baku at last and was en-route to the Ukraine. Now the time had come for Edgar to fulfil the expectations of the Russians to ensure that the communications equipment was utilised most advantageously. After leaving Tbilisi, a slow two-day train journey followed by a long truck drive

A Valentine tank as shipped to Russia via the 'Southern' route.

over what passed for roads in the Ukraine, he eventually arrived at an armoured vehicle base a few miles behind the front line.

Edgar digressed here a little and spoke about the Russian Army as he saw them at Tbilisi and on the Ukrainian front. The first thing that struck him at Tbilisi was the immaculately dressed officers usually of the rank of Major and above. By comparison, British battledress was very drab. It appeared to him then – and this was reinforced in the Ukraine – that the gap between Russian officers and other ranks, was almost unbridgeable.

A typical Soviet tank crew as trained by Edgar to install and use wireless sets in newly arrived British tanks.

Also, until officers reached the rank of Major, they were of little or no account, unless on special small party operations. Their views were rarely, if ever, sought. Whereas in British armed services they looked at a hierarchical structure, e.g. C.O., Staff Officer, Adjutant, Officers, RSM, NCOs, the Russian Army was quite differently structured. In lieu of staff officers, they had Political Commissars and almost all authority was vested in them.

Too much must not, however, be read into the political part. Yes, they were appointed by the Politburo, but they were also well versed in all things appertaining to the arm of the service to which they were attached. So in a typical armoured or infantry Regiment, you would expect to see the Political Commissar ranking as a Major or above with virtually the final say on battle plans. It could be said that no one in the Russian armed forces could look to advancement in his career, without catching the favourable eye of the Political Commissar. Having said that, Edgar had, in fairness, to say that all the Political Commissars he met were manifestly well up to their job.

Back to the Ukraine. In battle dress, without insignia, he stood out like a sore thumb and this was intended to be. He was on his very own. He sought out the Armoured Brigade's Political Commissar, who was well briefed about him, and enquired whether the communications equipment had arrived from Baku and was relieved to learn it had – at last!

Next Edgar showed the Political Commissar his compact transceiver (probably a Mk VII), and asked permission to set it up so that he could be in communication with London and Kuybeshev. He was told there was no problem so within a relatively short while, he was in contact with London and Kuybeshev and told them he was 'in business'.

Now came the tricky bit. He was expecting to use the experience he had gained with the 11th Hussars and the Tank Corps at Tidworth in 1933, i.e. to install and maintain mobile communication equipment. To this end he hoped to be working either in a small workshop of his own, or part of a larger workshop. All he was offered was a rudimentary shack in which to unpack his equipment, lay it out, test it and get it into working order. The shack was also his living and sleeping area and space was found for his mobile wireless link to London and Kuybeshev. (See Appendix 8).

There were now a great many organisational difficulties, principally due to the fact there were no Russian officers of authority on hand, in the equivalent of the Royal Signals, Royal Engineers, or Royal Army Ordnance Corps. Eventually, the Armoured Brigade's Political Commissar came to his aid and he saw that the brightest technical junior officers and senior NCOs were seconded to him for a month's training.

So the daily round began. Stripping equipment down, testing it, reassembling it and finally fitting it into tanks or armoured cars, as required. They usually worked from 08.00 to 20.00 daily, seven days a week. After two or three days it became obvious who out of the six potential instructors were going to make the grade and with further assistance from the Political Commissar, Edgar quickly put a team together.

Edgar here mentions a snag he encountered at the very beginning, and which went on right through his stay in Russia. It was the sheer impatience of an otherwise patient and placid race. Always, as soon as he, (and afterwards those he had taught), had installed a set in a tank or armoured vehicle, the Commander was for despatching it to the front. Edgar pleaded with them to allow him to complete the installation of at least two Troops, i.e. 6 or 8 armoured vehicles, and put the wireless sets in battle formation (this included using the equipment whilst firing live ammunition), before moving off to the front.

It reached the stage that he kept something back from each set and refused to allow them to become operational until at least two Troops were ready. Despite his best efforts, on two occasions, his Russian staff was intimidated into allowing single vehicles to go into action, as it were, piecemeal.

By the third week of December all the equipment sent up from Baku had been installed, Edgar's Russian team were relatively well up to basic maintenance and repair and he reported back accordingly to London and Kuybeshev. London informed him there was

little likelihood of further sets reaching Baku and thence the Ukraine before mid-January and he was given authority to return to Tbilisi.

T/34 the hugely successful Russian tank design, manufactured in great quantities in the Soviet Union. Over 55,000 were built up to 1945 and many thousands more after the end of World War II.

The Russians said he had to stay at the front and the Political Commissars were particularly adamant on the point. They capitulated only when they were ordered to do so by Kuybeshev. So the 21st of December saw him on his slow journey back to Tbilisi, where he arrived very late on the 23rd.

On the 24th fellow Mission members and Edgar compared notes and they then gave Colonel Way comprehensive reports on their work and all they had seen at the front. He was pleased that all the equipment transported via Baku and Teheran had been put to operational use, but angry with the Russians for not allowing him to visit all members of his Mission at various parts of the front. The Russians had confined his visits to artillery units, presumably because Colonel Way was an Artillery officer or maybe they were becoming aware of his other role?

Whatever the reason, Colonel Way was displeased. At the end of their briefing session, Edgar suggested they might invite Miss French, Miss English and Miss 'A.N. Other' to spend Christmas Day with them when, he hoped, the King's Christmas Day broadcast would come through loud and clear. This idea had also been in Colonel Way's mind as, during their absence, he had put together a few presents for the ladies. This brought them around to wondering what kind of a day the 25th would be for them.

As Edgar may have made clear, the Director of the Tbilisi Hotel made little or no effort to endear himself to them. Yes, their rooms were clean and comfortable, but the food was very basic and not much to their liking. For instance, breakfast was a type of semolina and Russian tea. The Director made sure any so-called extras were paid for on the spot. What would Christmas Day bring?

Well, if anything, breakfast was worse than ever, so-called lunch consisted of a bowl of soup and black bread. What more could the Director do to ensure their Christmas would be a day to be best forgotten?

After lunch they collected the ladies. They now called them 'our ladies' – and right up to recording the event here, Edgar recalled how lovely they looked. They had gone to so much trouble with their dresses, and really did the men proud. They all felt quite dowdy in comparison.

Back at the hotel they indulged themselves in a pre-dinner drink and again wondered what awful concoction would be presented as their evening meal. The hotel times for meals at the hotel were sacrosanct, they always had their evening meal exactly at 7pm. So, as well dressed as they could manage in Tbilisi, they proceeded to the dining room or, to be precise, a small room set apart for their use.

By now, with the return of Bruce Lockhart to Cairo, their Mission was down to ten – plus the three ladies. With Colonel Way at their head, they set off for their private dining room only to be stopped by the Director. They must wait, he said, all was not ready. A few minutes elapsed, the Director opened the door with an eloquent gesture and – what a surprise!

Their table, covered with a spotless damask cloth, was laid for thirteen places and overhead was a magnificent candelabra. The cutlery shone, as did the crystal glasses and the china was superb. The effect took their breath away. Then, as if that was not enough, waitresses appeared with twelve hollowed out small swedes with candles inside, and a larger swede similarly lit. The large swede was allocated to Colonel Way and the smaller ones to the three ladies and other members of the Mission.

Considering the dire straits Russia was in at that time, their Christmas dinner was excellent in every way. Edgar particularly remembered the hors-d'oeuvre, roast goose and vintage Georgian wines and champagne. What a meal.

They were in a mellow and expansive frame of mind when the Director strode in and demanded silence. He ordered that the brandy glasses be charged and then uttered words Edgar would never forget. In essence this is what he said: 'You think I am an ignorant Russian Georgian peasant. Well, I remember my mother and what she used to do at religious festivals. The small swedes are the twelve Apostles, the large swede is the Christ. I raise my glass to you and your Christ. Happy Christmas!'

They echoed 'Happy Christmas', embracing each other Russian fashion, and invited the Director to spend the rest of Christmas Day with them. They were all near to tears as they sang carols and songs associated with Christmastide.

Retiring to their briefing room, Edgar tuned his wireless set into London and they were uplifted on hearing the King's broadcast. Miss French confused George VI with Edward VII. Then the ladies regaled them with tales of Christmases in Victorian England and in the royal houses of Georgia. They asked if the men had a piano, the Director obliged and for the rest of the evening/night they were transported to a Victorian drawing-room and listened to songs of oh-so-long-ago!

Edgar could forever afterwards still see those lovely ladies entertaining them so charmingly. It was well into Boxing Day before they took them home – after they had declined the Director's invitation to spend the night at the hotel. Just prior to their leaving, Miss French asked them to kneel and they said the Lord's Prayer and the 23rd Psalm together.

New Year's Day saw all members of the Mission at the Headquarters of Red Army Command in Georgia. Rarely had Edgar seen such resplendent uniforms, much like a film set. The Commanding General introduced them individually to his officers, some with wives, and thanked them on behalf of the Soviet Government for the work they were doing. It was noticeable that only officers of the rank Major and above were at the reception. Everything was very friendly, good food and an abundance of wine and champagne. They had great difficulty getting away around about 5am. When the Soviets threw a party, it was certainly a great event.

Late January saw Edgar back at the front. This time, due to German advances, the base was many miles back from where it had been in November/December. Also, he and his

Russian crew were now subjected to much more frequent shelling and bombing. This pattern continued up to April, but having endured three or four weeks steadily retreating under continuous heavy fire, it was interrupted for Edgar by a few days at Tbilisi – waiting for the next load of equipment to arrive at the front.

By April 1942, the Germans were on the Caucasian borders, the British bases were almost untenable and both London and Kuybeshev said that no more supplies would be sent to Russia via the Gulf ports. They were told it was time for them to retreat to the safety of the Middle East.

Soviet troops following tanks across the battlefield.

Apart from Christmas Day and New Year's Day, the Soviets had hardly gone out of their way to make them feel welcome. The day before they caught the train to Djulfa/Tabriz, they paid their last visit to the war cemetery, and then said their emotional goodbyes to 'our' ladies. How Edgar admired them; they always remained for him a symbol of the best of our country.

So they took the train to Tabriz, the rail terminus, and from there they went on by Soviet army trucks over the mountains. This was in April and there was a tremendous amount of snow still around and Edgar remembered the Russian drivers were foolhardy. They were so glad when eventually they reached Zenjan where they were able to pick up the train into Teheran. At Teheran, they rested for two or three days and then caught a train down towards the Persian Gulf. From there they had motorised transport across to Basra. At Basra they took the metre gauge railway to Baghdad.

At Baghdad Edgar offloaded what equipment he had left. He had already left some in Teheran, and sought instructions as to what he was going to do next. Incidentally, the Embassy communication operator in Baghdad was one of those who had been on 'Main Line' in Athens, so they had quite a lot to talk about.

He then caught the main coach to Damascus. Now this was a coach that regularly went across the desert from Baghdad to Damascus. A long, long journey but with very interesting sights along the way. From Damascus he moved on to Jerusalem, and at Jerusalem he had instructions to catch the train to Cairo. He had quite a few bits and pieces from his visit, including a book by Georgia's famous writer, Rustevilli, called 'Nights in Tiger Skin'. It was a very lovely book presented to him by Veroshka Snegiriva.

Anyway this amongst other things was stolen on the rail journey, as he just couldn't keep awake. He had gone to sleep and thought the suitcase in his hand was safe, but the crafty thieves of the region were masters in their art. Edgar arrived at Cairo main station with just the clothes he was standing up in.

Michael 'Mike' Vivian met him there. He said he had an apartment in town, and that Edgar was to share it with him. They had a twin-bedded en-suite room with a small lounge. This was part of a large house owned by a Jewish family, who were very kind to them, and they enjoyed living there. One must remember that private accommodation was rare indeed, in the over-crowded wartime Cairo.

Mike Vivian was the son of Valentine Vivian the Deputy Chief of SIS, and Mike was later second in command at SCU11/12 in Delhi and Calcutta.

Mike Vivian told him that he had spent many days arguing with General Headquarters in Cairo. He said Edgar had, at one point, been declared a deserter and there had been a wide search over the Middle East looking for him. When he heard about the situation, he told them where Edgar was, and broadly what he was doing. However, it took them ages to accept it – because the operations of Section VIII were kept so secret – and 'need-to-know' was the order of the day, even right to the very top at GHQ!

A sequel – 16 Years Later

During Edgar's tour of duty at the British Embassy in Moscow from 1957 to 1958, he was in charge of communications. This was ostensibly in the DWS (Diplomatic Wireless Service), but in view of his long connection – he was still working for MI6. It was the practice for the Soviet Head of State to be invited to the Embassy for the Queen's Birthday Party, an invitation they never took up. It was, therefore, a great surprise when they were advised that Kruschev would be with them at the 1958 Queen's Birthday Party.

When he was introduced to him Edgar said, in Russian, that he had served on the Russian Southern Front in 1941 and 1942. At this, Kruschev jumped up from his seat, embraced Edgar strongly and kissed him on both cheeks. Edgar recalled he had the bluest of blue eyes. Afterwards the Ambassador, Sir Patrick Reilly, told him that Kruschev had been very pleased to meet him. Hitherto, Edgar had not mentioned being a member of the Way Mission to Russia.

Chapter 15

WORKING WITH AGENTS AND THE LRDG
1942-1943

So, after a short break, he took up his work again with ISLD in Cairo. This time it was to train agents who were a real mixture of races and nationalities; these included Arab, Asian, Greek, Italian, Yugoslavian, Romanian and Bulgarian. Once they were reasonably competent at operating in Morse and au-fait with our wireless gear and procedures, they would return to occupied territory as agents. Also, ISLD had 'turned' a Romanian born German agent captured in Cairo, complete with his equipment, but Edgar managed to work out his signal plans. He then made connection to – he assumed – Bucharest and he communicated with them for a short while.

However, there was obviously something wrong in his procedures because later their transmissions abruptly stopped and did not reappear.

He found it most interesting working with these agents. One he recalled in particular, was named Mohammed, and a sergeant in the Sudan Defence Force. He was a fine figure of a man, he spoke beautiful English, and Edgar came to regard him as quite a friend.

Following Erwin Rommel's victories in the Western Desert, the Army was being driven back towards El Alamein. It was thought

General Erwin Rommel commander of the Afrika Corps directing his forces. Their successful campaign was stopped at El Alamein by which time Edgar had already moved the ISLD agents' wireless station down into Kufra.

General Bernard Montgomery whose forces halted the advance of the Afrika Corps.

entirely possible he could go on to capture Alexandria just a few miles further, then Cairo and then occupy Egypt. As a result, it was considered safer, and politically wise, to move the GHQ of the Middle East Command from Cairo to Jerusalem. This obviously meant ISLD should go there as well – including Edgar and his agents' station and school. However, although the Main Line and agents' control wireless station were rapidly moved from Abassia to Jerusalem, they alao proposed that the agents' station itself be sent far south – down to the Kufra Oasis – the base of the Long Range Desert Group (LRDG). There, the wireless station could continue to keep in communication with those agents already in place, who had returned to German occupied territory.

It was decided that Edgar should first fly down to the Kufra Oasis, to ensure this remote area of the Libyan desert, far from the battle zones along the coast, was suitable for sending and receiving agent traffic and for use as a training base. (See LRDG appendix 9).

The flight to Kufra was via Wadi Halfa when he would most probably have flown in one of the two 'Waco' aircraft belonging to the LRDG 'Air force'. These had been found to be eminently suitable for the short landing strips and the conditions in the desert.

When he arrived at the LRDG base, he spoke to a Major who befriended him. Edgar explained his mission but the Major had received news of his visit and took him up to the fort. He found that it was ideally suited for an agent control station and flew back to Cairo to report his findings. There he recruited Henry Poole as an assistant and picked

up more wireless equipment. Henry was a very good operator and one to be trusted.

They then flew back to Kufra in a Lockheed Hudson with their wireless gear and together, they set up the ISLD wireless station. Life at Kufra was basic

Major David Stirling with one of the SAS patrols. Edgar becvame involved in a rescue operation of an SAS patrol after one of their raids.

in the extreme – absolutely no luxuries or comforts. Mostly, they slept outdoors adjacent to slit trenches into which they could roll on the sound of enemy aircraft. Over a period of many days they started to work to the many agents already in place – located in Italy, Yugoslavia, Bulgaria, Greece, Crete, and so on. At the same time, they worked on training of the agent 'recruits' now being sent to them.

It is said that Edgar took his team and equipment down to Kufra in an A28 Lockheed 'Hudson'. However, this picture is of a B34 Lockheed 'Ventura' in the desert, and the Ventura is almost identical to the Hudson. It was one of a number equipped by Mobile Construction department of Section VIII – at Tempsford airfield. It was very successful in making air to ground contact with our agents in Europe. It was in Egypt on trials and being connected with our unit, may well have been used to convey Edgar south.

This picture is especially important as it shows the Ventura with Wilf Lilburn standing in the centre – one of the remarkable Section VIII team, including my boss Dennis Smith, who devised the air-to-ground system called 'Ascension'. The Packard was one of the 'A Detatchment' sent to North Africa as an SLU but proved unsuitable when off-road.

Inset: One of the two American made 'Waco' aircraft of the so-called 'LRDG Airforce'. These versatile aircraft were one of the few able to take off and land in the tiny airstrips formed in the desert.

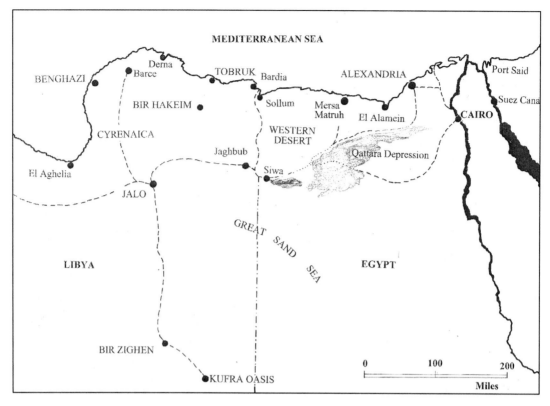

Meanwhile, Mohammed, the agent mentioned earlier, had been sent out to provide the wireless communication for a surveillance team that was sitting just outside Tripoli, by then hundreds of miles behind the German front line. The Eighth Army had just fought the first battle of El Alamein, where the German-Italian advance was finally halted.

After a time, knowing that the surveillance team had now left the area, Edgar became very concerned so he set out from Kufra with an LRDG patrol to look for Mohammed and bring him back to the base. Eventually, they found him in a small and remote hamlet. His hiding place had been down in a dry well and the rescue team brought him gently back to the surface. This fine figure of a man was now emaciated, covered with sores, and in a dreadful condition.

Edgar said, 'Mohammed, what have they done to you?' He said, 'Sir, what are my sufferings to compare with my King and Queen, who have been bombed in Buckingham Palace?' There was no answer Edgar could think of immediately to make in reply!

A desert patrol from the LRDG. Edgar travelled in identical vehicles whilst working out of the Kufra Oasis.

They set off intending to return with Mohammed to Kufra. Not far from Jalo they received a message telling them to do all possible to pick up members of David Stirling's SAS (Special Air Service) and their escorting LRDG patrol. Part of the Patrol continued on to Kufra taking Mohammed with them whilst the remainder, including Edgar, went on to find the survivors of David Stirling's party of SAS and the accompanying LRDG group. This they did – but at great cost.

A Long Range Desert Group patrol. At this time in the campaign, they were based in Kufra in the desert – over three hundred miles south from the Mediterranean coast.

The SAS had made what was being hailed as a wonderful raid on a principal airfield, destroyed many planes on the ground and raised a veritable swarm of hornets. The Germans and Italians were very angry indeed and the group were subjected to almost continuous air attacks.

Normally with Long Range Desert Group patrols, travel was by night, resting up during the day. But now, due to the obvious urgency, this was impossible and they had to travel in daylight. As a result, they were bombed and strafed mercilessly, losing both men and equipment. Edgar did not know how far they were away from Kufra, possibly 200 miles or so, when they arrived at what was an improvised airstrip.

This was one of the satellite strips that a Lieutenant Arnold had made during his time at Kufra. He was a magnificent man of Anglo-French extraction. He had gone out from Kufra making secret store depots and constructing satellite landing strips all over the area. He was later posthumously awarded a Military Cross for his gallant action in finding a breach through the Mareth Line, the German defensive line between Tunisia and Tripoli. This was, of course, after British forces had won the Battle of El Alamein and the 8th Army forces were pursuing the retreating German and Italian armies.

A patrol 'brewing up' and preparing a meal in the desert.

Meantime however, the LRDG patrols had been badly shot up, they sustained casualties and Edgar's main communication equipment was lost. All he had left was a transmitter and no receiver. His great friend in Cairo was Roy

Peacock, like himself a Captain in the Royal Signals, who had also trained agents. During their time together, they had made a habit, whenever they were near to their ISLD station in Cairo, to call in and listen for a few minutes, either on the hour or half hour – just in case there was any kind of SOS or urgent call. So Edgar opened up on his frequency and kept on sending their position, telling of their desperate situation and their exact location.

Often the patrol vehicles would become bogged down in soft sand.

The night wore on whilst they waited and waited and remember that Edgar was sending in Morse, with no idea if his transmission was being received. Then, and he always felt deeply touched about the following event; they heard the noise of an aircraft. It seemed unbelievable but yes, Roy Peacock had received his repeated messages and arranged for a rescue plane. They put on all the lights they could find to help its landing on this lonely desert airstrip. The plane landed safely, then took off again with all the wounded. They also packed on board all the others of their party they could spare and the plane returned safely to its base. Roy was awarded a Mention in Despatches for his part in the rescue.

Edgar continued on to Kufra with what was left of their party and stayed there working for a while. Then they had orders that the agents' station was to return to Cairo. By the time they were all safely back in Cairo, the 8th Army had won the battle of El Alamein and ISLD headquarters was also slowly returning to Cairo from Jerusalem.

The 8th Army were moving on through the desert, so the decision was now taken that the ISLD agents'control station, having moved back to Cairo from Jerusalem, would now move on to a place called Apollonia, which was just below Cyrene, at sea level.

There was a hospital in the town run by the RAF and an officer's mess. Roy Peacock and Edgar went along to the area, looked around, and found a delightful site for their station, overlooking the sea. The building also provided sleeping accommodation for them. So their wireless station was moved in and it proved to be a superb site, as they hoped, to be the main station responsible for all Italian, Cretan, Greek and Yugoslav agents. Of course, Edgar knew many of these agents having trained them in Cairo, with the assistance of Roy Peacock and Tommy Morton.

His brother Wallace had come up with them to Apollonia to be the station's wireless engineer. Edgar remained there for some time. It was quite an enjoyable location as there was no fear of being bombed or strafed and they came to know the RAF people very well.

One incident will illustrate the good relationship that existed between them all at this airfield. When someone was posted home – having finished their allotted time abroad – they used to have a big party or 'jolly' in the Mess. They were told there hadn't been a proper 'jolly' for ages because there was no alcohol available.

However, someone told Roy Peacock and Edgar that there was a place called Louisi Ratsa (or something similar) where there were numerous old wine vats. So the two of them set out with a collection of clean 'Jerry cans' to investigate. At first, they thought the vats were empty, but the locals told them there was still something in them. So they lowered the Jerry cans into the vats, filled quite a number up with the liquid contents and brought it back to the base. It was declared to be wine and quite potable. On reflection, Edgar thinks it must have been pretty awful but anyway it was all consumed and everyone thoroughly enjoyed themselves.

Then came the day when Wallace Harrison was told he was to return to the United Kingdom as he had served long enough overseas. Now being a member of Section VIII – that no longer meant to a Royal Signals army barracks – but to its HQ at Whaddon Hall in Buckinghamshire.

Shortly after Wallace left, a Major Pott, who had taken over from Wing-Commander 'Jock' Adamson, arrived at the base and told Edgar he was to go to Algiers.

As is well known, Eisenhower had landed in North Africa with both the 1st British Army and US troops. With the 8th Army heading west, and the Allied Armies under Eisenhower heading east from their landing points, they eventually cleared the Germans and Italians out of North Africa – taking many thousands of prisoners in the process.

Captain Tommy Morgan had already established a control station in Algiers. Edgar joined the team there and worked agent traffic. Then came the invasion of Sicily.

Chapter 16

THE INVASION OF SICILY AND STATIONS IN ITALY

Edgar and the work of Section VIII in Sicily

The continued Allied successes in North Africa lead to complete victory for the Allied forces and was the pre-requisite to the invasion of mainland Europe but instead of going through Yugoslavia as many expected, the first step was to be via Sicily. The decision to move into Sicily was taken at the Conference at Casablanca in January 1943. It was clear the Allies would not be strong enough to mount a cross-channel invasion of France for a year. On the other hand the Allies had very large forces stationed in the North Africa area facing Sicily.

The invasion – codenamed 'Husky' – started late on 9th July 1943 with the British 1st Airborne Division's 1st Air landing Brigade, circling in a huge aerial armada off Cape Passero. Their target-landing site was the open land outside Syracuse. The task was holding the Ponte Grande bridge over the River Anapo, until relieved by the British 5th

Division. Most of those in the invading force of just over 2,000 men were in 'Hamilcar' gliders towed behind various Allied aircraft. The gliders were made of plywood and sometimes referred to as 'flying coffins' and the aircraft that towed them as 'widow makers!' The battle of Sicily is more fully covered in Appendix 10.

Above left: General Sir Alan Brooke, CIGS (Chief of the Imperial General Staff) from 1941 to 1946.
Above right: Major-General Stewart Menzies, Head of SIS (or MI6) 1939-1952.

In April 1943 and some three months before the invasion of Sicily, General Sir Alan Brooke recorded a secret meeting held with 'C' (then Stewart Menzies) Head of SIS, at which he had been told that there were no British secret agents operating in

Sicily. At the time, some Allied intelligence gathering came from a most unlikely source, by reading the mail of Italian prisoners of war to and from their homes. Hundreds of thousands of Italian troops had been captured in the battles across North Africa and the Italian censorship was inept when it even existed. Italian forces did not use Enigma and so the major source of British intelligence – certainly of German military movements – was Ultra.

The interception of the German Enigma traffic was in the hands of many units in the Mediterranean, including special Army wireless groups. There were also SCU/SLUs operating in North Africa, with direct connection into Bletchley Park, via Windy Ridge in Whaddon although in some operations, traffic was relayed on from Cairo, or later from our Stations in Sicily and Italy. However, it is hardly surprising to read this official pronouncement to the effect that there were no 'British' agents in Sicily. Its towns and villages are very self-contained, due partly to the geography, but particularly to the parochial nature of their inhabitants. Any stranger 'planted' as an agent into such places, would certainly be leading a very dangerous – probably suicidal existence.

Max Houghting (seated) of SCU – the military cover for MI6 Section VIII.

However, Max Houghting, was one of Section VIII's wireless operators in the Mediterranean area and records in his story in 'The Secret Wireless War' of being stationed in Malta, and in contact with two agents in Sicily. He recently confirmed that was the case and was able to elaborate a little. Not surprisingly, he says one agent was working *'under great duress'* and the second was codenamed 'Cat' because, as they later discovered, he was based in Catania. He recalls 'Cat' was rather amateurish, since he would break from coded traffic into en-clair and attempt a conversation in Morse. Highly dangerous but he apparently survived!

More 'agents' (but with varied loyalties) existed in mainland Italy, particularly in the north of the country where partisan groups were active. Nevertheless, agents actually planted by MI6 were also in place in Italy and in contact with our ISLD stations.

Edgar, continued to work to agents. He later went back to Cairo and prepared to set up a forward station in Sicily. He collected material and instructions, then was flown back to Algiers and onwards to a landing strip near Syracuse in Western Sicily. He says he had

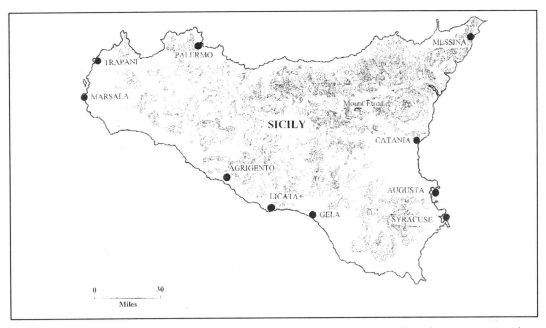

'a hairy time' but typically does not describe it in any other detail. However, other colleagues certainly did!

Soon after the start of the invasion of Sicily, Max Houghting, who was working at the ISLD HQ in Malta along with his colleagues 'Gravo' Graves, 'Midge' Middleton and Sergeant Griffiths (an engineer from Whaddon), were flown from Malta to the improvised landing strip at Syracuse in a Dakota. After a short time in tents, they set up a station in the top floor of a block of flats overlooking the harbour. Max said the continued German bombing of Syracuse harbour made the place like 'Hell!'.

Their main tasks were handling wireless traffic to and from Whaddon 'Main Line' station as well as passing Ultra traffic from Bletchley Park via 'Windy Ridge' at Whaddon out to Commanders. They were also, initially, making contact with our agents.

Generally, there were three main aspects of Section VIII's wireless work in the Mediterranean. Handling agents' traffic, Main Line traffic from Whaddon Hall, and the Ultra traffic for our Military Commanders from Bletchley Park – sent out via Windy Ridge at Whaddon. As we have seen, Edgar had been very closely involved in the Ultra traffic in Greece and Crete. However, his main task, after his return to Cairo and his stay in Yugoslavia, was handling agents' traffic. That continued to be his main role when he went down to open the station in Kufra, then in Algiers before being sent to Sicily. However, there were occasions when a station would have to handle all forms of traffic, and the early days of the invasion of Sicily was an example. Max Houghting relates handling Ultra and agents' traffic from the station in Syracuse.

Edgar was already on the island before the party from Malta, having landed from Cairo earlier. One knows, from other reports, that the fighting was very fierce. Both the

Germans and Italians fought well – the latter probably because they were now defending their 'homeland' instead of tracts of North Africa that they had conquered before the war – under Benito Mussolini.

Edgar tells us they quickly established an "agents' station" and reports that he made contact with his agents in Italy, Crete, Greece, and Yugoslavia. He definitely says 'agents in Italy' but does not specifically say in Sicily. Whilst I think his reference to being in contact with agents in 'Italy' could be construed as including Sicily, we can definitely say that Max Houghting's report of his regular contact with agents – *actually in Sicily* – are contrary to earlier high-level statements by 'C' the Chief of SIS – Stewart Menzies.

Italy

It had long been the intention that the ISLD control station for the agents in Southern Europe would eventually be placed somewhere in Italy, as well as a 'Main Line' station. So far as initial Ultra traffic was concerned that would come over with the SLUs accompanying the Allied Commanders. It later included one SCU/SLU manned by Ray Small with a team from Whaddon, who had earlier been active in Tunis. After the subsequent invasion of Italy itself, the ISLD Agents' Station finished up being at Bari, where it remained until the end of the war. It was set up by Major Henderson but soon replaced by (then) Major John Bruce Lockhart, with Edgar becoming its Signals Officer.

A 'Main Line' station (also handling Ultra for Italy) was eventually established in Torre del Grecco, just south of Naples. In charge was Lt. Col. MacFarlane from Section VIII assisted by 'Jan' Ware who had been one of the Naval Petty Officers who had served the unit so well. They worked the Ultra traffic for Italy out to the various SLUs at Allied Army and Air Force Commands.

After the ISLD station was fully operational and contacts made, Tommy Morgan arrived and took over as Signals Officer and Edgar was told to return to Algiers.

There he found instructions awaiting him to hand over his work, proceed to Gibraltar and from there, return to MI6 Section VIII HQ – at Whaddon Hall.

He flew to Gibraltar, stayed there a few days and was invited up to the Governor-General's residence where he found Major-General McFarlane, who remembered him from his time at the Embassy in Brussels, before the German Blitzkrieg in 1940.

Their plane set off for home, flying all through the night, but when they arrived over England, it was absolutely blanketed by fog and the pilot expressed his concern about landing conditions. They

Ray Small of SCU (MI6 Section VIII).

managed to establish communication with the aircraft's base and they suggested there could be an airfield – either in Somerset or in South Wales– that might be fog free. With fuel getting very low, they found Western Zoyland in Somerset and made a landing there. The fog persisted so they spent that day and night there in the RAF Officers quarters, before leaving for the RAF airfield at Northolt.

There, Edgar contacted Wing Commander 'Jock' Adamson at Whaddon Hall – via the switchboard in SIS HQ at 54 Broadway in Westminster – and he sent a Packard down to pick him up. Eventually, Edgar returned to the bosom of the Section VIII family at Whaddon Hall. It had been a very much longer period abroad than the six months Richard Gambier-Parry had suggested when he had set off for Greece to make contact with his brother, Major-General Michael Gambier-Parry in Athens, back in September 1940.

Anyway he was thankful to be back home.

Chapter 17

TEACHING AT WHADDON AND THEN INTO EUROPE WITH SCU8

It was at the end of 1943 that he arrived back home to Whaddon Hall. He naturally wondered what role they now had in mind for him. After a brief leave, he found he was assigned to Squadron-Leader 'Dickie' Matthews, who was in charge of training at the wireless training unit – known as SCU7. This was to one side of a small military camp, near the village of Little Horwood, some three miles from Whaddon. The main camp was known to all, as 'Gees' after the name of its owner, a London building contractor.

There, together with two other Captains from the Royal Signals, Bill Wort and 'Dusty' Miller they instructed men in Morse and wireless procedures, in preparation for the invasion into France and Germany. Some men were RAF aircraftmen recently sent to SCU7 from 'Chicksands'. This was one of the 'Y' service listening units, monitoring German wireless traffic that was then sent on to Bletchley Park for deciphering.

Above: Squadron Leader 'Dickie' Matthews RAF in charge of SCU7 – the Morse and wireless training wing of SCU (MI6 Section VIII).

Edgar was not sure at first how they would be employed, but anyway they were obviously 'surplus to requirements' at Chicksands. He soon found out his task was to quickly get these RAF 'recruits' into shape as wireless operators. Whilst they were very willing, he felt they were not really up to SCU wireless operator standards. During the early part of 1944, they managed to get them up to a reasonable proficiency and in sufficient numbers, to supplement the Army signalmen of the Royal Signals that had already had already been trained at SCU7 by Squadron Leader 'Dickie' Matthews' teams.

These signalmen had mostly been billeted at 'Ashby's' – a house requisitioned for the purpose in the ancient town of Stony Stratford – some seven miles north of Bletchley Park. The mobile wireless units formed for 'D-Day' were designated 'SCU8' for the invasion of Europe on 'D-Day' and beyond into France and Germany. These stations were known as 'SCU/SLUs' and would be receiving the Ultra traffic from

Left: Ashby's in Stony Stratford about four miles from Whaddon Hall and the billet for those undergoing wireless training at SCU7.

Bletchley Park via Windy Ridge at Whaddon, then directly into the HQ of the various Allied Military Commanders in the field.

Alongside each wireless vehicle – Guy 15cwt vans for the British and Canadian sectors and Dodge ambulances for the US forces – would be a matching vehicle devoted to cyphers. The cypher vans were manned by RAF cypher personnel provided by Bletchley Park. However, they were apparently trained in their skill in cypher work in several different locations around the country.

Left: The landing taking place on the beaches of France.
Right: An SCU/SLU in the field in Europe. This was the one attached to General Patton's 3rd US Army and Wilf Neal was one of its SCU wireless operators. (See 'The Secret Wireless War' chapter 25). However, it was typical and utilised a converted Dodge ambulance as the mobile wireless station. Edgar Harrison and his team would have been in an identical outfit with General Simpson's 9th US Army.

Invasion fleet off Normandy beaches discharging troops and material – June 1944.

The specially designed mobile wireless units were being constructed in the Mobile Construction Unit based near the exit gate of Whaddon Hall – see Appendix No. 11.

In addition to improving their Morse speeds, Edgar also instructed the airmen from Chicksands in Section VIII procedures. Then he took 'groups' of them over to France and allocated them, as required, to various Commanders. However, he apparently went with one group himself to work with the American 15th Army under General Simpson and at the end of the war found himself at Halten.

Chapter 18

PROVIDING ULTRA WIRELESS
COMMUNICATION FOR WINSTON CHURCHILL

During the war, Mr. Churchill held a number of conferences in the Middle East area, sometimes with Heads of Government and sometimes with military leaders.

The Prime Minister travelled to these by plane from London usually accompanied by his Foreign Minister, Military Advisers, his personal doctor, valet, secretary and others. Space on the plane was therefore somewhat limited. Rather than add a wireless operator and all his equipment to the complement on

A USAF B24 Liberator Bomber. One was used by Winston Churchill for much of his travels although considerably altered into virtually an air liner.

the flight all the way out from London, it was decided to use a member of Section VIII already stationed in Cairo. The Prime Minister was insistent he should constantly have up-to-date information on the Ultra traffic emanating from Bletchley Park. Quite apart from keeping up with intelligence reports, this enabled him to indulge in 'one-upmanship' – particularly in the presence of Roosevelt and Stalin.

All relevant Ultra traffic from Bletchley Park, and any 'Top Secret' messages intended for Mr. Churchill when he was abroad, was always handled by MI6 (Section VIII) – via its wireless stations in Whaddon Village. Edgar was usually chosen as the Section VIII wireless operator for Mr Churchill when he was in the Middle East region.

Only one of the Conferences was recorded in some detail, that with the President of Turkey. This took place at Mersin in eastern Turkey in January 1943, after the victory at

Mr. Churchill's personal Liberator B24 – named 'Commando' with Winston in the cockpit!

El Alamein. Edgar's passport was taken away and he was told it was to have a visa put in but not told for which country. Some hours later, in the greatest secrecy, Edgar was told the Prime Minister was flying to Turkey for a meeting with the Turkish President at which he was to provide the communications.

In just a matter of hours his passport received a Turkish visa, he then tested his 'agents' small suitcase transceiver (undoubtedly a MkVII), made at

Whaddon Hall. Then shortly afterwards and now in civilian clothes, he was emplaned in a Dakota, and on his way. The weather was dreadful, torrential rain and they were forced to land at Tel Aviv for a few hours awaiting a lull in the storm. Eventually the pilot, Group-Captain Huddlestone, decided they had to go on and thankfully the sun came out as they landed at Adana – close to the meeting place in Mersin – and drew up alongside the Prime Minister's plane.

With utmost haste Edgar was whisked, MkVII suitcase in hand, to the Presidential train, a mile or so away, in a secluded siding. He was allocated a large compartment on the train and inside was the 12-volt car battery that the Embassy had been asked to ensure was fully charged. This was, after all, the sole source of energy for his transceiver.

He earlier noticed there was a signal gantry adjacent to his compartment and within minutes, he had climbed up the gantry, secured one end of his aerial to it and led it back to his transceiver. He was now in contact with both Cairo and London.

An early MkVII transceiver wireless set in a suitcase. – The type used by Edgar Harrison on his journeys with Winston Churchill.

The later MkVII/2 'Cash box' version of the MkVII – just possibly used in later conferences.

Mr Churchill at talks with Mr Inonu President of Turkey in the Presidential train at Mersin

Going along the corridors of the train he duly reported personally to the Prime Minister that communication had been established with London and Cairo. Mr. Churchill kindly said, 'You are a remarkable signaller Harrison.' During the two-day conference, signals were exchanged with Cairo and London, but Edgar managed to snatch a few minutes sleep from time to time.

Obviously he needed to eat and he allowed himself about a thirty-minute break each time. When he first entered the restaurant car for a meal, there were high-ranking Admirals and Air Force Officers at various tables. He was beckoned over by General Alexander to share his table. He said, 'we Army chaps have to stick together.' Edgar had meals with him on three later occasions on that trip. He comments 'Such a nice man.'

The evening before they left Mersin the Prime Minister emphasised the importance of receiving an up-to-date weather forecast from Cairo before they would leave for their next destination. Cairo informed Edgar the forecast would be transmitted to him at 08.00 and he ensured the Prime Minister was made aware of this.

As promised, the weather forecast was received at 08.00. Edgar delivered it to the Prime Minister personally and, much to his surprise, he had hardly returned to his compartment before the train lurched forward and they were off. There was no time to recover his aerial, so it was left dangling from the signal gantry. He felt there was a measure of impatience in getting the train underway so soon after delivering the weather forecast. The train halted a little way from the airport where the Prime Minister's plane was ready for take off.

The Dakota that had flown Edgar up to Mersin having returned to Cairo, he was found a place on Churchill's rather crowded plane. Anyway, they took off, their destination being still unknown to him. An hour or so later they were over land and commencing a descent. Soon they were flying over a large town, which he recognised as Nicosia from a previous association with the island. The Prime Minister enquired fairly loudly the name of the town, but this elicited no reply from his illustrious staff and colleagues.

Edgar – as a humble wireless operator and not wanting to appear a 'know all' felt it was not up to him to speak. However, the Prime Minister enquired again, even more loudly. He then plucked up courage to say, 'I think it is Nicosia, which the Cypriots know as Lefkosia'. Winston was obviously not in a good mood, he said, 'What do you mean you *think* you know Harrison? You either *know*, or do not *know*!'

They had a one-night stopover at Nicosia where accommodation was provided for him in the Officers Mess. He had a nice room and after lunch lay down for a while. He had been without proper sleep for seventy-two hours. The Prime Minister and his advisers went to attend a mini Conference with all the senior Allied Officials in the Middle East area. Edgar's sleep however, was interrupted by what sounded like small-arms fire. It was in fact a heavy hailstorm falling on the tin roof. As if that was not enough, he was awakened very early the next morning by banging on his door and shouts of 'Time to get up!'

It was hardly daylight, but General Montgomery had issued an order that all troops – across the whole Middle East – needed to have exercise before breakfast. Almost needless to say, Edgar remained in his bed until it was time to leave. They flew on to Cairo, where he said his goodbyes and returned to nearby ISLD, complete with his suitcase set.

The following day one of the Prime Minister's secretaries came to see Edgar. He said the 'old man' had noticed his name was not included in the party returning to London. Edgar explained that he was based in Cairo. A short while later, the secretary came back to say, the

The Teheran Summit held between Stalin, Roosevelt and Churchill. Edgar was the MI6 wireless operator in attendance.

Prime Minister would like Edgar to purchase a few small items for loved ones at home, and he would ensure they were delivered. This he did and the family duly received his gifts. He so much appreciated this thoughtfulness on the Prime Minister's part, whilst carrying the burden of prosecuting the war on his shoulders.

Edgar records that he was in attendance at five 'conferences' – Cairo, Mersin, Nicosia, Teheran and Yalta but he offered no further details of them in his files or papers. I have tried to deal with this problem in Appendix 12.

However, he did relate an anecdote connected with another of them. Apparently, he was travelling in Churchill's plane on the outward flight, when a snack lunch was served. After the meal, a tray of cheeses was produced and later the steward asked what Edgar thought of the selection. He remarked that given the British Prime Minister was travelling it would have been nice to have some British cheeses, instead of foreign cheese.

Lo and behold, on the return flight, all the cheeses offered came from Britain. Clearly, the steward had accepted his recommendation.

Many years later Edgar received an invitation to attend Sir Winston Churchill's funeral. Unfortunately he could not accept, as he was on his way to take up a new appointment with the Diplomatic Wireless Service in Singapore.

Mr Churchill's Liberator 'Commando'.

Appendix 1

Bletchley Park, Enigma and Whaddon Hall

Throughout the book you will find continued reference to two places – Bletchley Park and Whaddon Hall. Both played a great part in Edgar's wartime story and to his career as the Principal Signals Officer of the DWS – the Diplomatic Wireless Service – the post-war wireless communication division of the Foreign Office.

He had of course, never heard of Bletchley Park until January 1940. Then, whilst travelling as ordered on a train from London to Northampton, he read from a letter which had been contained in a sealed envelope instructions to leave the train at Bletchley Station '...*where you will be met....*'. This phrase was used in the same way to many hundreds joining these most secret of organisations.

Bletchley Park.
Bletchley, (now a part of Milton Keynes) was then a small town some 50 miles north of London that straddled Watling Street – the old Roman Road – listed by then as the A5. It also had Bletchley railway station nearby – on a major line from London to the North and to Scotland.

Bletchley Park was to the west of the town just beyond the station and had been the home of Sir Herbert Leon, a wealthy benefactor to the town. The Mansion was built in the Victorian period and stood in considerable grounds. It came up for sale in 1938 and was purchased by Admiral Sir Hugh Sinclair the Chief of the SIS – the Secret Intelligence Service. He was known only as 'C' in the media and to the public.

Bletchley Park Mansion

Sinclair wanted the property for what he described as his 'War Station'. It was in effect, to be a place of safety for various divisions (or Sections) of SIS (MI6) – then all based in the headquarters at 54 Broadway in Westminster near the centre of London. Like others, he realised that war with Germany was becoming inevitable and would lead to air raids on the scale being seen in Spain in its Civil War.

Soon after it was purchased, the newly formed MI6 (Section VIII) under Richard Gambier-Parry, now responsible for all SIS communications, built a wireless station for themselves into the tower of the house that became known as 'Station X'. Later to a few, that title was quite erroneously given to Bletchley Park itself. The work was carried out by the leading Section VIII engineers, and included Claude Herbert a retired Chief Petty Officer in the Royal Navy, who had just purchased a house for his family in Bletchley. This station was completed in the latter part of 1938, and then another station was built into a hut near to the Mansion. This station became known as 'Hut 1' simply for being the first and only hut at the time!

With the outbreak of war, a previously rehearsed evacuation from Broadway took place. The largest area of the Mansion and some outbuildings, were devoted to a division known as GC&CS the Government Code and Cipher School. It occupied much of the ground floor whilst various other 'Sections' were allotted upper rooms. Sinclair was already aware of the huge potential in breaking the codes encyphered by the Germans on their Enigma machines and suddenly, with the outbreak of war, funds were made available for expansion.

Throughout the pre-war period GC&CS were constantly handling low-grade cyphers and their cryptanalysts producing intelligence reports from them. GC&CS had no wireless facilities of its own and had to rely upon the Services – Army,

Above: Close-up of the Enigma rotors.
Enigma in battle. Guderian directing the Blitzkrieg across France command in 1940 from his command vehicle. The Enigma machine is at the bottom of the picture.

RAF and Navy – to intercept the German military Enigma wireless traffic that its work later depended upon. These became collectively known as the 'Y Service'.

Fortunately, these were mostly well-established organisations based in various parts of the country and providing their own accommodation. The Navy intercept stations were at Scarborough and Winchester, the Army who were monitoring the Enigma traffic were initially based at Fort Bridgeland, Chatham and the RAF had an intercept station at Cheadle.

Many books exist telling of the actual breaking of the Enigma codes. My first book 'The Secret Wireless War' has a short chapter called 'Enigma, A Brief Outline,' and that is sufficient to indicate the reliance placed on its total security by the German Army, Navy and Air Force. In addition the German Abwehr, their Secret Service, used their own version of an Enigma machine to encypher their wireless traffic.

Again, the breaking of the Enigma machine codes is well documented but it meant that GC&CS had a rapid need for linguists, mathematicians, secretaries, filing clerks, drivers, catering staff, nurses, and personnel of all kinds. As scores of new personnel arrived at Bletchley Park there was obviously pressure on the limited space at first available. This lead to the other divisions of SIS being moved out nearby at first, and then some a considerable distance away. Initially the break-neck expansion of GC&CS was housed in the famous pre-fabricated timber 'Huts' erected in the grounds near the Mansion and they were followed by many more of brick construction – but that was some time into the future.

The output of the cryptanalysts was marked 'Secret' – 'Top Secret' and 'Most Secret' but signals intelligence messages (or 'Sigint') intended for the eyes of our Military Commanders in the field was later and increasingly, marked 'Ultra'. That has now become the generic word to describe the intelligence output from Bletchley Park.

At first, like the others, Section VIII had been allotted rooms in the upper floors of the Mansion and one was given over to the SIS's own cypher Section headed by the imperious Miss 'Monty' Montgomery – irreverently known by some as the 'Mongoose'. Though she continued to work on SIS cyphers at Bletchley Park throughout the war as an autonomous section she later had private offices in Hut 10.

So secret was her work that she was given living accommodation within the security zone of Whaddon Hall in a house called 'The Chase'. She was transported back and forth daily to Bletchley Park by a Packard saloon belonging to Section VIII.

Section VIII was another division of SIS – and one closely associated and vital to the 'Enigma' process – that had become responsible for disseminating the Signals Intelligence (Sigint) output of Bletchley Park in the form of wireless messages. This too had outgrown its allocated space at Bletchley Park and so a new home was found for it.

Whaddon Hall

On 12th September 1939, Hugh Sinclair approved the leasing of Whaddon Hall, a fine Georgian mansion in Whaddon village, some six miles west of Bletchley. Whaddon Hall then became the headquarters of MI6 Section VIII under Richard Gambier-Parry. Work started at once to move the staff, workshops and wireless operations from Bletchley, including those recently transferred from Barnes, Woldingham and the senior personnel left in London.

The front of Whaddon Hall 1939

The move was to include the wireless station in the tower of the Bletchley Park Mansion and the station in Hut 1. Following the erection of aerials, the transfer of actual wireless equipment was started in November and completed by early 1940.

Enigma Machine

The wireless operational side was first based in the Hall with aerials on the roof but 'Hut 1' from BP was soon housed in permanent buildings in the fields directly opposite the front of the Hall where they carried out the same role and became known as 'Main Line'. The extensive rooms of the Hall now contained the offices, whilst the staff of every level, were billeted locally into requisitioned houses in Whaddon, or in private homes or pubs in the surrounding villages.

The widespread stables and coach houses around the stable yard of the Hall became the first engineering workshops under Bob Hornby, 'Spuggy' Newton, heading up wireless engineering, and Charlie West in charge of the metal workshop. Further stables became the home of the increasing wireless stores. These moves were taking place whilst wooden huts to house the workshops were urgently being built in the grounds of the Hall, between the stable yard and the road outside leading to Stony Stratford.

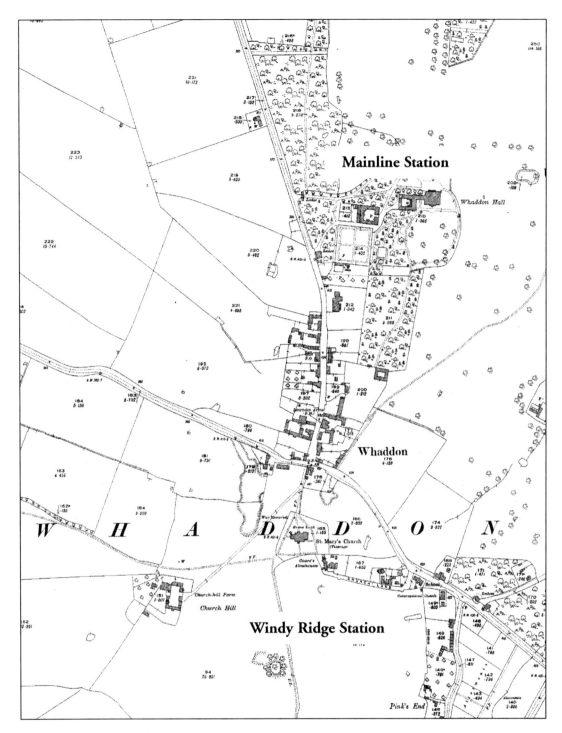

Whaddon Village is dominated by Whaddon Hall (at the top of the map) and it had associated out-buildings across the village such as Kennels for the Whaddon Chase Hunt. Richard Gambier-Parry built his 'Main Line' wireless station in the fields a short distance in front of the Hall and the 'Windy Ridge' station – handling the Ultra traffic – built on a ridge of land close to St. Mary's Church.

Section VIII had a variety of roles that expanded rapidly. Probably the most important was the dissemination of 'Sigint' especially to our Military Commanders in the field when it was designated 'Ultra'. A new station built in a field alongside Whaddon Church handled this vital traffic. The field is the high point of the ridge running through Whaddon village and rightly earned the name of 'Windy Ridge' and that name was applied to the station.

'Windy Ridge' was to play such a tremendous part in the war passing Ultra messages through to our Army Commanders giving them up-to-date intelligence on the German intentions. It deserves a bigger part in the history of the war.

Another and major task was the interception of Abwehr traffic (the German Secret Service wireless traffic) and this was undertaken by two sub-divisions. 'SCU3' based at Hanslope, some ten miles to the north of Bletchley and 'RSS' based in Barnet but with more intercept and D/F (Direction Finding) stations later built across the country. They also had a network of 'VIs' – **V**oluntary **I**nterceptors who had been pre-war wireless amateurs. As amateurs, they were used to listening to weak Morse traffic from across the world, thus their skills were superior, in this regard, to the newly trained service personnel who manned the normal 'Y' service stations.

In addition to intercepting the Abwehr traffic, SCU3 at Hanslope and the RSS organisation (including its VIs) intercepted the SD (Sicherheitsdienst). The SD was Himmler's own secret intelligence department of the SS and responsible to him alone.

Both SCU3 and RSS, as sub-divisions of Section VIII, came under the direct control of Lt. Col. 'Ted' Maltby who was deputy to Brigadier Richard Gambier-Parry.

In the nearby villages around Whaddon Hall, Section VIII constructed wireless stations that had nothing to do with the 'Ultra' traffic arising from Bletchley Park, or the Embassy traffic (covert or otherwise) handled by 'Mainline'. These stations were located in fields near the villages of Nash and Calverton (Upper Weald) and the powerful transmitter for both stations was located just outside Calverton village itself. The sole task of Nash and Weald (and the later station up at Forfar in Scotland) was to contact SIS agents abroad and particularly in occupied Europe.

From the very start, Richard Gambier-Parry had set out to design and manufacture his own wireless sets for SIS use. That had commenced at Barnes and then continued at Woldingham. He later provided wireless training facilities in the SIS agent school – at 23 Hans Place just behind Harrods.

By 1941, extensive wireless and metal workshops had been built in the grounds of Whaddon Hall between the stable yard and the road to Stony Stratford. These huts also contained R&D laboratories continuing the units' lead in modern wireless technology.

Some of the many other roles undertaken during the war – by this most secret of units – are mentioned in Appendix 11.

Appendix 2

Richard Gambier-Parry and the SCUs (Special Communication Units)

Richard Gambier-Parry Head of MI6 Section VIII

Richard Gambier-Parry was born in 1894, the son of a wealthy architect and attended Eton. In the First World War he served as an officer with the Royal Welch Fusiliers where his older brother Michael was already a captain. Richard was wounded twice and mentioned in despatches. Later in the war he was seconded to the Royal Flying Corps (RFC) where he obtained his wings as a fighter pilot. The RFC later became the Royal Air Force.

He had a keen interest in wireless and held an amateur wireless licence in the very earliest days as shown by his licence number 2DV. Licences after 1926 had to show the prefix 'G' (for Great Britain) thus his became G-2DV. From 1926 to 1931 he was the BBC's Public Relations Officer before joining Philco UK Limited as General Sales Manager. They were the British division of Philco – the giant American wireless company.

Hugh Sinclair needed a man to bring SIS communications up-to-date for the war that he knew was looming. Richard Gambier-Parry was selected, no doubt on a recommendation by Colonel Stewart Menzies. He was Head of the

Stewart Menzies who became 'C' Head of SIS in 1939 on the death of Admiral Sir Hugh Sinclair.

Police complex at Barnes in West London, containing the SIS wireless station. The aerials can be seen and also the tall mast of the nearby Marconi factory making communication equipment.

military arm of the SIS organisation and was to become 'C' himself on the death of Hugh Sinclair in November 1939.

Richard Gambier-Parry's huge task was to transform an ill-equipped and ill-trained organisation and make it ready for war. Throughout that year he sought skilled wireless engineers and wireless operators to modernise the communication capability of the Secret Intelligence Service. Incredibly much passing of secret information was done by cable, messengers, or even by the public telegram system – at least it was in code!

The Royal Navy had played a part earlier but the wireless traffic was relayed from shore station to ship to ship, and so on across the world to HMS Flowerdown at Portsmouth – before being relayed to Barnes and thus into SIS hands. Gambier-Parry was determined to have control of the traffic in his own hands. I am given to understand the Lords of the Admiralty were not best pleased to have this long-held role taken away from them.

Gambier-Parry had inherited the existing SIS wireless station that was tucked away in the large complex of buildings behind the Metropolitan Police station, alongside the Thames at Barnes, in West London. More space was required and fortunately a small printing factory a few hundred yards away, again facing the Thames, became vacant in 1938 and it was purchased immediately. It was called 'Florence House' and was rapidly turned into a modern wireless receiving station.

To begin with they continued to use the Post Office transmitter at Daventry connected by landline and/or HMS Flowerdown. However, they soon acquired 'Funny Neuk' a large bungalow in remote Woldingham in Surrey and built a fully equipped wireless station and small workshop in it. The site was high in the Surrey hills and the aerials they erected were well sited for world wide transmission. Interestingly, the two names on the 'Funny Neuk' electoral role in 1938 were Hugh Sinclair who was 'C' and Wilf Lilburn another ex-Philco member of Section VIII.

Florence House fronting the River Thames at Barnes, purchased in 1938 to replace the station in the Police complex, some four hundred yards away.

'Funny Neuk' a World War I building in a quiet part of Woldingham in Surrey intended as the transmitting station for Florence House.

Above left: Harry Tricker one of the Chief Petty Officers recruited into Section VIII.

Above middle: Harry Tricker as a Lieutenant in the Royal Corps of Signals. All the Chief Petty Officers were appointed Majors – by the end of the war.

Above right: Jack Saunders another of the Naval party but sadly he was lost in a Westland Lysander on returning from occupied France.

As a result of his energetic work in that first year, Gambier-Parry had established a new wireless facility, entirely under his own control, not dependent upon cooperation with the Post Office or Royal Navy. He was able to transmit and receive worldwide and now had to build up wireless stations in various Embassies to enable covert messages to be passed in complete secrecy.

In late 1938 Gambier-Parry's team built the wireless station in the tower of the Bletchley Park mansion and by early 1939, was able to communicate with the established agents in Europe, often using the new agents' sets manufactured by his teams in Barnes and Woldingham. The engineers involved included Bob Hornby, 'Spuggy' Newton, Bob Chennells, Wilf Lilburn and Charlie West – all of these had come from Philco. At the same time he was again fortunate. A number of very skilled Chief Petty Officers in the Royal Navy wireless division were just 'finishing their time' in the Navy.

Their Commanding Officer at HMS Flowerdown, the Navy's wireless station in the hills above Portsmouth, was trying to talk them into signing on again. One of them, Claude Herbert had just left and was already working as a civilian operator for the Foreign Office at Embassies in Europe. Section VIII knew of him through a visit by Bob Hornby – who was impressed with his skills.

Claude Herbert told Hornby that there were other Chief Petty Officers thinking of signing on again for further service with the Navy. It should be noted that several Royal

Navy shore establishments had wireless/telegraphy staff that were already involved in interception and some limited covert work. Edgar Harrison, then in the Royal Corps of Signals, was doing just that in China until 1937. Like Edgar, all Navy W/T operators needed to be both telegraphists and wireless engineers, the perfect combination for the tasks they would be required to perform in Section VIII.

As a result of quickly arranged meetings, Gambier-Parry was able to recruit them into his infant unit. They included Jack Saunders, Charles Bradford, Harry Tricker, and Jan Ware. All of them brought just the right skills he needed in Section VIII at that time. Incidentally, each of them eventually became a Major in the Royal Corps of Signals, and a real asset to the organisation.

At that time, MI6 was divided into ten parts or 'Sections' [See Appendix 15] and Gambier-Parry was Head of Section VIII. It covered the various aspects of wireless communications that was later to include the dissemination of Ultra traffic arising from Bletchley Park. That particular aspect of Section VIII's work – distributing Ultra to Commanders in the field – was handled by SCUs in conjunction with Special Liaison Units (SLUs), [See Appendix 3].

Richard Gambier-Parry, was later joined by what might be called the 'founding fathers' of the rebuilt Section VIII. It included 'Ted' Maltby, John Darwin and 'Micky' Jourdain who had already held military rank and wore appropriate uniform. Now as serving MI6 officers they could automatically resume their services rank but Richard Gambier-Parry was made a full Colonel.

The German Blitzkrieg on 10th May 1940, ended the so-called 'Phoney War'. It quickly lead to the defeat of the Allied forces and the evacuation of the BEF from a series of Channel ports – mainly Dunkirk. An early German invasion into Southern England seemed possible so it was decided that the rest of the staff of the rapidly expanding Section VIII of SIS could not continue to appear as civilians. Gambier-Parry decided to 'militarise' Section VIII and so Special Signals Unit No.1 (SSU-1), was set up in late May 1940.

Military Intelligence at the War Office were approached and it was agreed that the Section VIII civilians could be enrolled ostensibly as members of the Royal Corps of Signals – although they

This is the 'Main Line' wireless station in the fields in front of Whaddon Hall. It handled Embassy traffic including covert. Edgar's wireless messages on behalf of Winston Churchill for London would go via here. It handled considerable amounts of SIGINT traffic as well.

were not to be paid from army funds. At first, the unit was called 'Special Signals Unit No. 1' (SSU1) but it was felt that the word 'Signals' might give the game away. In 'The Story of the SLUs' (PRO HW3-145) – written presumably by Winterbotham in 1945 as part of the History of Bletchley Park – it is suggested that the change of name was prompted by other units assuming that SSU stood for Secret Service Unit!

So, in the climate of the heightened concern with secrecy, the word 'Signals' was changed to 'Communications' and so finally in 1941 it became 'Special Communication Unit' (SCU) and that name remained until the end of the war. By 1945 there were fourteen SCUs around the world.

The dissemination of 'Ultra' messages was certainly the most important part of the many roles of Section VIII. Ultra messages were sent from Bletchley Park to the War Office, Admiralty, Air Ministry and other service control centres directly by teleprinter. That intended for overseas, and especially our Commanders in the field, were more usually sent by teleprinter to Whaddon, for onward transmission by wireless.

There, messages for the SLUs (Signals Liaison Units) in the field were routed through the SWG – 'Special Wireless Group' based in huts on Windy Ridge near Whaddon Church. Others went out via the 'Main Line' station in the group of huts in the field – directly opposite Whaddon Hall.

This traffic for our Military Commanders would be received in a mobile wireless unit where the operators were provided by SCU. These would be parked near the SLU vehicle containing a cypher crew, often RAF personnel provided by Bletchley Park. The combined unit was known as a SCU/SLU and kept as close as possible to the Field Commander within his HQ.

Additionally, the unit provided the specially adapted wireless vehicles and personnel for all these mobile SCUs, and the wireless stations to route the traffic to them, such as Cairo, Delhi, Calcutta, etc.

Almost equal to the dissemination of Ultra in importance, was the interception of the German secret wireless traffic, such as Gestapo and Abwehr by SCU3 and RSS. This traffic was of immense benefit to the SIS, the military and politicians. SCU3/RSS built up a wide network of intercepting wireless stations and direction finding (DF) units to locate the source of these signals. They used amateur wireless operators (Voluntary Interceptors or VIs) based in their homes that intercepted and reported this most secret traffic to RSS HQ at Barnet. They were all sworn to secrecy but their special skills had come pre-war from constantly listening to fellow amateurs from across the world. Those with this very special skill at picking up weak signals were sometimes referred to as 'DX-ers'.

Opposite:
Daily Orders for Special Signal Unit No. 1 dated 25th July 1940. It shows Colonel R. Gambier-Parry as its Commanding Officer and contains a number of men enlisted including my father H. E. C. Pidgeon. Most of these men were in Section VIII and not paid by the Army.

DAILY ORDERS PART I
by
Colonel R. Gambier-Parry.
Comd., S.S.U. No.1.

Issue 20 dated 25 Jul 40.

96. POSTINGS.

    (a)   The following personnel have been enlisted at Whaddon and are posted as shown :-

N.Y.A.	Sigmn.	Holden. G.E.	Workshops.	18 Jul 40.
"	"	Sweet. C.F.	H.Q.(S.O(SS)).	"
"	"	Kempton. H.A.	Workshops.	"
"	"	Morrow. I.A.	H.Q. Tailor.	"
"	"	West. C.W.	Workshops.	20 Jul 40.
"	"	Hill. J.	"	"
"	"	Roberts. J.G.W.	"	"
"	"	Pidgeon.H.E.C.	H.Q. (S.O.Tech).	"
"	"	Castleman.H.J.	Workshops.	"
"	"	Ord. J.T.	"	"
"	"	Lax. D.	"	"
"	"	Bromley.K.A.	Trg Group.	22 Jul 40.

    (b)   The undermentioned Officer arrived in the Unit :-

    Lieut. C.M. Harrison.   Signal Officer.   24 Jul 40.

    (c)   The undermentioned are posted to H.Q.C. todays date :-

    2585609 Sigmn. Hooper. K.W.J.
    2308091   "   Thompson, C.

    The undermentioned are posted as operators to Training Group :-

    2091512 Sigmn. Parrish. J.C.
    4742065   "   Hodgson. A.
    4445433 L/Cpl. Wilkinson. R.

    The undermentioned are posted to Transport w.e.f. todays date :-

    2337575 Sigmn. Dally. W.S.
    2337797   "   Calvert. W.

97. ATTACHMENTS.

    The undermentioned are attached to the Scottish Command, w.e.f. todays date :-

    2321782 A/U/L/Cpl. Nisbet. I.S.
    2580926 Sigmn.   Cullen. W.N.
    T/131018 Dvr.   Howie. W.

    The undermentioned are attached to the Admiralty, w.e.f. 26 Jul 40 :-

    2308091 Sigmn. Thompson. C.
    2585609   "   Hooper. K.W.J.
    T/66188 Dvr.   Broadfoot. J.

Richard Gambier-Parry's teams also provided all our wireless communication with the MI6 agents abroad across Europe – as well as making the wireless sets they used. In Britain, the wireless stations listening-in to agents in France, the Low Countries and Denmark, were operated from Weald and Nash wireless stations, both near Whaddon village. Those in Norway as well as other parts of Scandinavia, by the SCU station at Forfar in Scotland.

Overseas, he had wireless stations – sometimes mobile – that dealt just with our agents in Bulgaria, Italy, Sicily, North Africa, Yugoslavia, Crete and the general Mediterranean/Eastern Europe area. That was often Edgar's role at the station in Cairo that he later evacuated to Kufra in the Libyan Desert, when Rommel threatened to overrun Alexandria and Cairo.

Whilst these are two separate aspects of Section VIII, the top operators of the unit quite often had to switch from one role to the other. For example, in Greece and Crete, Edgar and his two colleagues were handling SIGINT traffic for our Military Commanders. When Edgar arrived in Cairo, he later had a spell helping out on the Main Line and Ultra traffic – to and from Whaddon – before later becoming responsible for the agents' station at Kufra.

Section VIII designed and built wireless sets to make FM (voice) contact to agents on the ground from aircraft flying some distance away. This enabled agents, perhaps with slow Morse ability, to pass their messages rapidly with less chance of German DF (Direction Finding) units tracing their location. The system was called 'Ascension' and constantly up-dated by the R&D (Research and Development) department at Whaddon.

Richard Gambier-Parry supplied wireless operators in our Embassies in neutral countries. For example, Bill Miller who worked covertly in Tangier.

A wide range of 'Agents' sets' were designed and built both at Whaddon Hall and in a small secret 'factory'. This was tucked away in the transport depot in the military camp, at nearby Little Horwood.

A number of selected Motor Torpedo Boats and Motor Gun Boats, were based in ports like Brixham and Dartmouth, and used to ferry agents and their gear to France and the Low Countries. They were fitted with Section VIII wireless to keep contact with the agents there and some for interception.

Wireless stations across the world were designed and supplied from Whaddon. The list and diversity of the work carried out by Section VIII is seemingly endless and a credit to a quite brilliant man. Whilst heading up this extensive and vital organisation, Gambier-Parry was very approachable and kept a keen sense of humour. However, what endeared him to us most was the knowledge that he always gave full support to his staff – however junior.

Little wonder, that at the unveiling of his portrait at Bletchley Park in 2001, Edgar told the audience Gambier-Parry was loved by us all. A sentiment heartily endorsed by the wartime colleagues present.

In 1946, Gambier-Parry's SCU organisation that had served SIS and the country so well, was largely reformed by him as the Diplomatic Wireless Service, part of the Foreign Office, and initially took on many of its functions.

Edgar Harrison was later to become the Principal Signals Officer of the Diplomatic Wireless Service with responsibility for its wireless communications throughout the world.

When he retired after the war, Richard Gambier-Parry sent a portrait to many of the Section VIII and DWS staff and signed it 'Pop'. Throughout the war he had signed his 'Christmas Message to the Editor' of our House Magazine 'Stable Gossip' – in the same way. I presented a copy of the portrait and a eulogy to the Bletchley Park Trust in 2001 and it hangs in the hall of the Mansion. When I unveiled it I asked Edgar to join me and we performed the ceremony together.

Appendix 3

SLUs – (Special Liaison Units) – the Voice of Ultra

The outgoing intelligence from Bletchley Park to the Admiralty, War Office, Air Ministry and Cabinet Office was at first sent by despatch riders and then by teleprinter on dedicated landlines. However, these dealt only with the fixed headquarters buildings in London and were not suitable for the wider distribution becoming necessary. The early breaking of some codes meant that intelligence gathered needed to be forwarded to the British Expeditionary Force (BEF) in France and the only logical way was by wireless.

The Army naturally had a wireless facility attached to its HQ. However, whilst the established Army wireless service was not very sophisticated it also had the drawback of opening the new, and highly secret SIGINT from Bletchley Park up to a wide 'audience' – untutored in its vital importance.

Section VIII purchased a Dodge car and this was fitted out by 'Spuggy' Newton with a complete W/T system and sent to the HQ of the BEF at Wachines in France on Tuesday 14th November 1939. A second car was made ready shortly afterwards and sent to the RAF Advanced Air Striking Force at Meaux.

The operations carried out by these cars were hugely successful, and thus proved the importance of taking the signals intelligence or SIGINT (later referred to as Ultra), gleaned at Bletchley Park – directly to the Military Commander in the field and thus bypassing the 'usual channels' and communicating with Whaddon Hall and thence to Bletchley Park.

The SLU officers, Robert Gore-Browne and Humphrey Plowden, were from SIS and that attached to the RAF was Squadron Leader F. W. (Tubby) Long. The wireless operators came from Richard Gambier-Parry's Section VIII – by now based at Whaddon. One was certainly Bill Sharpe. The second was initially, to the best of my knowledge, Arthur 'Spuggy' Newton.

The skill acquired in fitting out the cars for the British Expeditionary Force in 1939 was of great benefit to the Whaddon engineers in 1940 after the miracle of Dunkirk. With the rising threat of invasion in the summer of 1940 from the victorious German Army now right along the French coast, Gambier-Parry acquired some seventy Packard motorcars. These came from Leonard Williams Limited who were Packard's UK distributor based in Brentford, west London. At Whaddon they were fitted out as mobile wireless stations. The aim was to provide continued SIGINT communication to the War Office, the Air Ministry and the Admiralty, if they had to move in the event of invasion.

Group Captain Fred W. Winterbotham gave the name 'Special Liaison Unit' or 'SLU' to all units (mobile or static) handling Ultra traffic coming out of Bletchley Park. Colonel Stewart Menzies (newly appointed 'C' following the death of Admiral Sir Hugh Sinclair), had charged Winterbotham to ensure the total secrecy of the information being disseminated by Bletchley Park.

To begin with, there were a number of fixed SLUs in the UK, such as at the Admiralty, the War Office, the Air Ministry and at RAF Fighter Command. Fixed SLUs were gradually established in other centres of operations like Cairo (where Edgar helped out at times), Delhi, Comilla in Assam, and Kandy in Ceylon, Delhi, Brisbane and so on.

A Packard Sedan SLU of our 'A Detachment' sent to North Africa in early 1941 to take Ultra traffic directly into the field headquarters of our Military Commanders. They proved unsuitable off-road.

The staff at the wireless stations serving these SLUs was frequently SCU personnel and that was certainly the case, to my personal knowledge, in Delhi, Kandy and Calcutta. These continued to be referred to as SLUs but in the case of Delhi, Kandy and Calcutta were part of SCU11/12. This latter unit was under Lt. Col. Bill Sharpe who had been one of the wireless operators on the first mobile SLUs sent to the BEF in France in 1940.

Several Humber shooting brakes were purchased in Cairo and they replaced the Packards in the desert.

One other SLU to be mentioned was at Kunming in China where SCU had a wireless station under Tom Kennerley. The traffic to and from Kunming was sent via Calcutta, who relayed it on to Whaddon. Tom's small station also handled and trained agents to operate in the area and dealt with their traffic.

Some of the static SLUs received their information directly from Hut 3 in Bletchley Park via the BP teleprinter operators and others via the Section VIII wireless station at Windy Ridge.

However in the days following Dunkirk and under the threat of invasion, most also had a mobile support team from SCU1 (at Whaddon) as a wireless backup in case the Ministry was put out of action, or had to move in the event of a German assault eventually reaching London. Edgar was in charge of such a mobile wireless unit sent to Western Command in Chester in a Packard, shortly after his return from Dunkirk.

The information from Hut 3 would in that event, go out via the BP teleprinters to Section VIII's W/T station at 'Windy Ridge' near the Whaddon village church and then to the SCU team at the designated SLU. The SCU team in the 'Dugout' in St. James Park supporting the War Office SLU – is an example of where this backup existed.

A Guy SLU utilising a standard Army 15cwt wireless van stripped of its normal wireless gear and fitted with SCU equipment – including an HRO receiver and a MkIII transmitter.

It is known that in 1940 a mobile SCU unit was sent from Whaddon to the Admiralty, as a mobile emergency support W/T station to receive traffic from Bletchley Park. (SSU1 Daily Orders Part 1. dated 25th July 1940, Item 97 Attachments). Further afield, the wireless communications at SLUs were almost always run by SCU personnel.

The SCU/SLU of General Patton's 3rd US Army in Europe after 'D-Day' with its converted Dodge Ambulances, one containing wireless gear and the second the cypher unit.

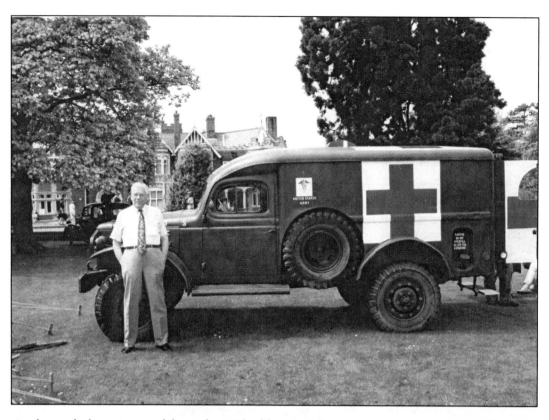

Dodge ambulance just as delivered at Whaddon Hall for conversion into an SCU/SLU. This standard US ambulance was photographed at Bletchley Park in 2003 with Wilf Neal – one of the original wireless operators with General Patton is standing in front.

Things were quite **different** for military commands abroad where the SLU clearly had to be mobile, moving with the Army or Air Force Commanders. When a mobile SLU was attached to a command, such as in North Africa, Sicily, Italy, and later in the re occupation of Europe, the unit consisted of two parts.

The SLU cypher crew in one vehicle would be coupled with an SCU wireless van, where the staff actually handled the Ultra message. RAF personnel usually manned the cypher element and SCU personnel ran the wireless telegraphy element. These were men from the Royal Corps of Signals at Whaddon/Little Horwood. However, occasionally staff for an SCU could come from the RAF and this happened in North Africa with the 'A' Detachment from SCU1 in 1941 where initially they used Packard sedan motorcars, then later Humber estate cars.

General Patton

Operators were drawn from skilled RAF wireless staff and George Hainsworth is an example of where RAF personnel were 'recruited' – in his case by Jan Ware of Section VIII in Cairo. Others were Max Houghting and 'Midge' Middleton who were recruited in Malta by Bill Furze and made members of SCUs. Although they continued to receive their RAF pay, their money was 'made up' from Section VIII funds.

General Montgomery in France after 'D-Day' with General Bradley commanding the 1st US Army to his right, and General Dempsey commanding the 21st Army Group to his left. All three had an SCU/SLU providing them with ULTRA right in their Headquarters. In the case of Bradley the wireless van would be a Dodge Ambulance whereas both Montgomery and Dempsey had Guy 15cwt vehicles. These were all converted by Mobile Construction at Whaddon Hall.

So as time went on, these mobile SLUs were more often referred to as 'SCU/SLUs' to indicate that they were mobile units.

There was an SCU/SLU wireless facility provided on General Eisenhower's train in his travels around the various military commands across Britain, shortly before D-Day. Great Western Railway (GWR) apparently supplied the coaches, which after the war I believe, were used as reserve coaches for the Royal Train. Although I cannot be certain, I suggest that an agent's set would have been sufficient to provide General Eisenhower with a wireless facility for that short period within the UK, working traffic to and from Whaddon. Any wireless operator would certainly have been from SCU.

General Montgomery also travelled extensively by train across Britain in the weeks before the invasion of Europe. He visited the British, Canadian and US forces that were to come under his command on D-Day. His four-coach train was known as 'Rapier' and was effectively his travelling HQ and had a flat car with it to carry his Rolls Royce. Under the circumstances, it is highly likely that his staff would have had a secure wireless channel on the train for him.

Appendix 4

The Sino-Japanese War in the 1930s

Because Edgar was in China in the 1930s and travelled extensively, it is therefore essential to try to give the reader an outline of the complex political situation that existed in the country at the time. Also to explain the growing threat of all-out war, as opposed to the various battles that in spite of sometimes being on a huge scale, were classified as 'Incidents'.

However, before doing so, it should be noted that whilst Edgar was travelling extensively over the whole region on interception work for the 'Foreign Office' (but almost certainly for SIS), Naval Intelligence was conducting interception of the Japanese forces' and diplomatic traffic on a larger scale over the same period. The intelligence gleaned from all sources was discussed at joint meetings at Broadway but perhaps Sinclair wanted his own input into the information being gathered?

It should be remembered that the Royal Navy had provided our intelligence for many years through the Naval Intelligence Division (NID). The Head of the Secret Service had been a Naval Officer. right back to 1909 to the days of Admiral Sir Edmund Slade, later it was Admiral Alexander Bethell, followed by several other Admirals and Vice-Admirals up to the appointment of Captain Mansfield Smith-Cumming RN, who was the first Chief of the Secret Intelligence Service (SIS) more widely known as MI6.

He died in 1923 and was followed by yet another Naval Officer, Admiral Hugh Sinclair who presided over the SIS until his death in November 1939. Then the Cabinet met under the Prime Minister Neville Chamberlain to agree a replacement. Most wanted to appoint Colonel Stewart Menzies – Sinclair's Deputy and Head of the Military Division of MI6 – to follow him. This was generally agreed but the First Lord of the Admiralty Winston Churchill, insisted on Admiral John Godfrey, Head of NID, being given the post. Yet another Naval Officer!

This dispute in the Cabinet surprisingly went on for nearly three weeks – dithering in time of war – over a most important and urgent appointment. In the end, Stewart Menzies was appointed to the position and proved most successful. As an aside, he became close to Winston Churchill who found him an invaluable aide after he became Prime Minister in the dark days of 1940.

The second Sino-Japanese War (July 7th 1937 to September 9th 1945) was a major war fought between the Republic of China and the Empire of Japan, both before and during World War II. Although the two countries had fought intermittently since 1931, full-scale war started in earnest in 1937 and ended only with the surrender of Japan in 1945.

Casualties caused during the attack on Shanghai when British troops were killed as reported by Edgar.

Japanese troops invaded Manchuria in what they described as the 'Mukden Incident'.

Heavy casualties and damage was caused throughout Shanghai during the Battle of Shanghai.

Bomber aircraft of the Imperial Japanese Army Air force over Shanghai in 1937.

The Japanese invasion in 1937 was a strategic plan made by the Imperial Japanese Army as part of its large-scale plans to control the Asian mainland. Before 1937, the two sides fought smaller engagements in the so-called 'Incidents'. The 1931 invasion of Manchuria by Japan is referred to as the 'Mukden Incident'. The last of these was the Marco Polo Bridge Incident of 1937, marking the official beginning of full-scale war between the two countries. From 1937 to 1941 China fought alone, the Rape of Nanking being well documented. After the attacks on Pearl Harbour, the second Sino-Japanese 'Incident' merged into the greater conflict of World War II.

The word 'Incident' was used by Japan as neither country actually declared war on the other. Japan wanted to avoid intervention by other countries such as the United Kingdom and particularly the United States, which had been the biggest steel exporter to Japan. The American President Mr. Roosevelt would have had to impose an embargo due to the Neutrality Act – had the fighting been included as part of a world war. In Imperial propaganda however, the invasion of China became 'Holy war'. In 1940

Japanese forces in the field.

Prime Minister Konoe thus launched the 'League of Diet Members Believing the Objectives of the Holy War'. When both sides formally declared war in December 1941– the name was replaced by the 'Greater East Asia War'.

The internal situation in China was very complex. Leaving aside 'War Lords' who still held sway over parts of the country, there were two main factions involved in a civil war. At the same time as the Japanese were making incursions, the Chinese Nationalist Party or Kuomintang (the KMT) headed by General Chiang Kai-Shek were locked in frequent battles with the huge communist forces led by Mao-tse-Tung. They had fought and lost some bitter campaigns but to avoid complete annihilation by the Nationalist forces, several of the communist armies escaped to the North and to the West over the period 1934-1936.

General Chiang Kai-Shek,
Chairman of the Nationalist Government of China.

These became famous as the 'Long Marches' and although the estimates differ about the actual distances covered – it was in the order of 6,000 miles over the most difficult terrain. The several communist armies involved eventually came under the command of Mao-tse-Tung and Chou En-lai. Strict orders prevented looting along this extraordinary march and that endeared the troops to the local towns and villages they passed through – so unusual for Chinese forces who normally seized what they wanted.

These communist forces later joined hands with the Nationalist armies to fight Japan – the common enemy – but after World War II the Red Army (or People's Liberation Army) became the government of China under Mao.

Appendix 5

Greece and Crete
The first use of Ultra on a large scale,
showing its immense possibilities and its weaknesses.

Edgar was involved from the start in this early use of Ultra. He was sent in late 1940, to join the British Military Mission under Major-General Michael Gambier-Parry in Athens. There he set up a station entirely dedicated to Ultra and assisted two other Section VIII operators who were handling 'Main line' traffic to London. He fitted out a car as a mobile wireless station – effectively a mobile SLU to take SIGINT right up to the Commanders in the field.

However, we should go back to 1939 when the United Kingdom had extended a guarantee of military aid if Greek territorial integrity was threatened. At the time the threat from Germany developed, the British were deeply committed to fighting in North Africa and could not spare many military units or war material to assist Greece. British public opinion was inspired by the way the Greeks had repulsed the Italians, and Prime Minister Winston Churchill thought it would be dishonorable not to aid the Greeks.

The first British help to Greece were a few RAF squadrons under Air Vice-Marshal John d'Albiac, sent to aid the small Royal Hellenic Air Force in November 1940 while with the consent of the Greek government, British forces occupied Crete on 3rd October, releasing the 5th Cretan Division for the Albanian front.

Early on, however, voices were raised among the British Commanders against committing some of the already limited forces from North Africa to mainland Greece, a move that would weaken both their position in Libya, and would be of limited help to the Greeks. The Greeks, on the other hand, were afraid of provoking the Germans, although they were determined to resist an invasion, if it came. At a meeting with British Commander-in-Chief Middle East, Archibald Wavell, in January 1941, Greek Commander-in-Chief Papagos requested nine fully equipped divisions for the Greco-/Bulgarian border. When Wavell answered that he could dispose of only 2-3 divisions, the offer was turned down, as the force was totally inadequate and would only hasten German intervention. Churchill, however, by now hoped to recreate the Balkan Front of World War I with the participation of Yugoslavia and Turkey, and sent Anthony Eden and Sir John Dill to the region for negotiations.

At a meeting in Athens on February 22nd between Eden and the Greek leadership, the decision to send a British Commonwealth Expeditionary Force was taken. Already German troops had been massing in Romania, and on 1st March 1941, Bulgaria joined the Axis. As German forces began crossing the Danube into the country, the German invasion was now imminent.

Hitler was determined to ensure his southern flank was covered and the occupation of Greece was required to secure that for him. That meant moving through Yugoslavia where he hoped his tripartite agreement, just signed in Vienna on 25th March by Prince Paul its Regent, would enable him to use the railway system to transport his armies rapidly across the country to reach the Greek borders. However, there was a coup d'état two days later and it was clear the country would not abide by the agreement.

Furious at the changed situation Hitler ordered the German High Command to put together an Army to fight its way through Yugoslavia and occupy Greece. It consisted of 29 divisions and 2000 aircraft were allocated to support it. It was a massive Army – one might say – overkill.

As a result of the earlier moves, 58,000 British, Australian, and New Zealand troops were sent to Greece in March 1941 in Operation Lustre, comprising 6th Australian Division, New Zealand 2nd Division and British 1st Armoured Brigade Group. The three formations later became known as 'W' Force from their Commanding General Henry Maitland Wilson. Although earmarked for Greece – Wavell kept the Polish Independent Carpathian Rifle Brigade and the Australian 7th Division – back in Egypt because of Erwin Rommel's successful thrust into Cyrenaica.

Eden however failed to entice Turkey to abandon her neutrality, while Yugoslavia, under intense German pressure, prevaricated, until it joined the Axis on March 25th. Almost immediately, a successful Serb-backed, pro-Allied coup was launched on March 27th, but it came too late to allow for the creation of the coherent alliance that Churchill had hoped would come to pass.

'W Force' had only begun to settle in their defensive line when news of the German invasion came. The outcome of initial clashes with the Germans at Vevi was not encouraging and the rapid advance of the Panzers into Thessaloniki and Prilep in Southern Yugoslavia greatly disturbed Wilson. He was now faced with the prospect of being pinned by the invading Germans operating from Thessaloniki while being flanked by the German XL Panzer Corps descending through the Monastir Gap.

This necessitated a retreat, initially to the Aliakmon river and then to the narrow pass at Thermopylae, where the Germans broke through again on April 23rd. Although the

Greek forces put up a truly heroic fight, the German massed guns and tanks were simply too much for them and after the surrender of the Greek First Army it was not long before it was decided to pull out.

After some brief holding actions on the Peloponnese, most of the Greek and British Commonwealth forces were evacuated to Crete and Egypt. The 5th New Zealand Brigade was evacuated on the night of 24th April, while the 4th New Zealand Brigade remained to block the narrow road to Athens, which was dubbed the 24 Hour Pass by the New Zealanders. On 25th April, Anzac Day some 5,500 Australian troops of the Australian 19th Brigade were evacuated from the beaches at Nafplio by three ships HMAS Perth, Stuart and Voyager. The evacuation of about 43,000 soldiers was completed on April 28th mostly from Kalamata where the final stand on Greek soil was made. The evacuation was heavily contested by the German

Athens occupied by the Nazis. A German armoured vehicle patrols in the city under the shadow of the Parthenon.

Luftwaffe, which managed to sink a number of troop-laden ships. The Germans managed to capture around 8,000 Commonwealth troops who had not been evacuated, while liberating many Italian prisoners from POW camps.

The General now appointed to command in Crete was General Freyberg, a New Zealand VC from World War I and greatly favoured by Churchill.

The Air Officer Commanding in Crete, Group Captain Beamish, had been in receipt of 'Orange Leopard' Signals (the 'OL' Series), from Bletchley Park via the Section VIII wireless station at Windy Ridge at Whaddon from 28th April. This was shortly before Freyberg's appointment as General Officer Commanding Crete, and they arrived regularly into May. All these gave the most detailed account of the German battle plan for Crete and the likely order of battle.

General Freyberg VC Commanding the Allied Forces in Crete during the attack by German Paratroops.

General Freyberg's personal gear being taken ashore in Crete.

Allied troops arriving in Crete just prior to the German 'Operation Mercury'.

The detail ran to whether certain areas of waters would be mined or not, whether airstrips would be bombed or not. Later Ultra signals told them – for example – that the 7th Fliegerdivision plus Corps troops of the 11th Fliegerkorps would seize Maleme and Candia (Heraklion) airfields, and detailed the mountain troops that would accompany them. How Italian torpedo boats would protect the sea-going German and Italian vessels containing troops and supplies – and so it went on!

Day after day, the most detailed information was given then one – OL2168 on 7th May caused a mistake by the HQ. It said, inter-alia Flak units, further troops and supplies mentioned in OL2167 are to proceed by sea to Crete. Also three mountain regiments thought more likely than 3rd Mountain Regiment.

Allied HQ thought that 3 mountain regiments were coming in *addition* to the 7th Parachute Division and 22nd Air Landing Division.

Numbers of troops of all kinds were listed, the weight of supplies being lifted in, number and types of cargo planes available plus the number of journeys they could make, number of bombers, number of fighter planes, and in OL 2/302 on 13th May, a summary of the entire German plan from their Day One onwards. It spoke of an attack force of 30,000 to 35,000 men, of which some 12,000 would be a parachute landing contingent and 10,000 landed by sea; where supplies were being assembled, and even details of an Italian tanker being loaded with fuel at Piraeus to ensure fuel supplies. The numbers actually used were considerably less but

German paratroops in Greece preparing to board Junkers JU52s – prior to the attack on Crete.

nevertheless it was a formidable force especially as it consisted entirely of highly trained, motivated and confident troops.

On 19th May, OL 12/370 told of a meeting at 08.00, of officers commanding German Airforce that would take place at Eleusis aerodrome on the 19th May. It went on to say that an attack on Maleme aerodrome would take place and that day (19th) was the assault day – minus one.

It is impossible to read all the information in the incoming Ultra messages, and then believe that the combined Allied forces were not prepared for the landings to take place in the locations, so clearly described.

The Bren Gun Carrier is a very lightly armoured – and open top – tracked vehicle. There were a few of these on the Island but they should not be confused with tanks!

There were about 42,000 troops in Freyberg's command and contained British, New Zealand, Australian, Greek and Cretan troops. It is right to point out that some of the units were not of full strength; most were battle weary who had to improvise a defence after they had been evacuated from Greece. They had only two or three weeks to recuperate and reform. The number, also included some Greek soldiers of varying capability, but there were already Cretan guerrilla forces assembled that could – and did – give a good account of themselves during the battle of Crete, and later during the occupation.

However, they had no tanks, their anti-aircraft guns had been put out of action and little transport. All that could be evacuated from Greece had been sent back to North Africa.

There were several fundamental flaws. General Freyberg was not told the source of the intelligence, so he was not aware of the Ultra operation and believed the information came from agent sources. Wavell had given Freyberg the impression of a 'well-placed spy' and Freyberg never doubted the story, or guessed that the information came from intercepts of actual German military signals. He thus failed to understand the Chief of Staffs Signal telling him on 9th May, that '...*so complete is our information that it appears to present a heaven sent opportunity of dealing the enemy a heavy blow...*'.

He was also bound up with the messages about sea-borne landings. He ignored specific on-the-ground reconnoitering that had pointed out that the area was not conducive to landing on the beaches, without proper landing craft – and of course the Germans had none.

The following will demonstrate the element of confusion created for our Commanders. The Naval Intelligence Division (NID) at the Admiralty received its signals direct from Bletchley Park. They normally passed them on to qualified recipients as 'from a usually reliable source' or 'from an unknown source'. However, the First Sea Lord was Admiral Sir Dudley Pound and he had different ideas. When the message came down from Bletchley Park that the intended attack was to be on Crete on May 20th, the signal informing Admiral Cunningham Naval Commander-in-Chief in the Mediterranean was first sent to Pound. He had the signal altered from Crete to read '...Malta, Crete or Cyprus'.

One must ask how a Naval Fleet Commander could possibly use intelligence that mentioned targets – hundreds of miles apart? Fortunately, Cairo also relayed the original message to the Naval HQ at Alexandria and fortunately the target was properly identified.

A synopsis to his excellent book – 'Crete, the battle and the resistance' – by Anthony Beevor says:

'The invasion from the air, unique in the history of warfare, turned into the closest run battle of the war. The slaughter of the German paratroopers on the first day by New Zealand, Australian and British troops was so great that if one more platoon had still been in place on Maleme airfield the next morning, General Student would have been forced to admit defeat. For the first time Ultra intelligence played a key role. But how General Freyberg, Churchill's favourite hero from the First World War, handled that information and the battle itself remains controversial.'

Whilst this talented General may have misused some of the information presented to him, it is difficult to understand why, a full General of the highest reputation, should not have been told the source of the intelligence he was receiving. How much more credence he would have given the messages, if he had known he was looking at actual German signals, and not the intelligence gathering of an agent!

Later on, our Military Commanders, at Army Command level were told the source of the information, if not the entire story of how it was obtained and analysed. How very different the outcome of the battle of Crete might have been – if only General Wavell had been able to tell General Freyberg the true source of Ultra during their meeting.

German bombers create havoc on Allied shipping in Suda Bay making all movement of men and material near impossible.

Now look at the situation on the ground. In spite of the numbers of Commonwealth and Greek troops under Freyberg's command he was short of material of all kinds. Many of the troops had left Greece with only their rifles and side arms; food, wireless communications and ammunition were low. Creating 'W Force' in the first place and sending it to the aid of Greece had left Wavell unable to spare more men from operations taking place in Cyrenaica. He certainly could not furnish the air support, material and transport needed. Apart from anything else, the harbours and

German paratroops landing on Crete from JU52 transport aircraft.

airports were mostly on the north coast of Crete under threat from air attack from the newly acquired German airfields in southern Greece.

Freyburg's reading of the 'Ultra' messages perhaps put too much emphasis on the mention of seaborne invasion and he felt sure the Allied Naval Forces would be unable to secure them from attack along that extensive coast. As a result, he dispersed his limited troops to ensure a 'seaborne landing' would not succeed. However, the signals clearly spoke in great detail of an airborne landing and as such they were limited to the airfields to bring in supporting equipment, ammunition and food for the lightly armed parachutists. Nevertheless, it is clear he did not sufficiently protect Maleme airfield and it was an obvious target for airborne troops. On the second day the Germans were able to secure a toehold and flew in aircraft with the ammunition and reinforcements so desperately needed.

In the event, the information provided by Ultra is clearly of limited use if the Generals in command of the Army in the field, do not know the true source or integrity of the knowledge, or have the military strength to respond to it. The messages received from Bletchley Park should have led to the first major defeat of the German Armies and in spite of the horrendous difficulties he faced, Freyberg might have succeeded. However, it is wrong to blame him alone for the situation that had arisen.

Convoy evacuating troops leaving Suda Bay for Alexandria.

These Ultra messages were being received by wireless in Greece, and later in Crete, by three men, Edgar Harrison, 'Dinger' Bell and 'Curly' Meadows.

I have in my possession a copy of the SIS 'Station Code Book' and it lists all the code numbers for each country. This belonged to Col. 'Micky' Jourdain one of the founding fathers of Section VIII who hoped he might be chosen to become Deputy to Richard Gambier-Parry. In the event, he was asked to leave for reasons explained in 'The Secret Wireless War' but before his departure, he gave Norman Walton (then his assistant) his SIS Station Code Book. In 2001 Norman allowed me to take a copy and the main list is illustrated. The last entry is in July 1940, so I suspect Jourdain left MI6 Section VIII soon after that date. It should be remembered that these SIS code numbers were a most closely guarded secret at the time.

You will see from Jourdain's list for example, that 38000 is Warsaw, and 23000 is Toulouse. The first two figures indicate the country – thus 17000 is Cairo. The Head of Station (the head of SIS at that location and usually the PCO – Passport Control

The most secret 'Station Code Book' belonging to Col. Micky Jourdain. The code for each city is shown there and for example – Athens is listed as 41000 described in the Firm as '41 Land'.

MALTA. *Month*					*Month*			ATHENS.	
49. Day	Time of Arrival	Departure		REMARKS	Day	Time of Arrival	Departure	REMARKS	**41.**
JONES 1	49950				1	41450		C.P MEADOWS	
O.St.√ 2					2	41951		J. M. BELL	
3					3				
4					4				
5					5				
6					6				
7					7				
8					8				
9					9				
10					10				
11					11				
12					12				
13					13				
14					14				
15					15				
16					16				
17					17				
18					18				
19					19				
20					20				
21					21				
22					22				
23					23				
24					24				
25					25				
26					26				
27					27				
28					28				
29					29				
30					30				
31					31				
Form E. 5 (estasignus).					Form E. 5 (estasignus).				

This shows the two MI6 (Section VIII) wireless operators stationed in Athens 41950 C. P. ('Curly') Meadows and 41951 J. M. ('Dinger') Bell.

Officer) is shown as 100 so would be designated 17100. However, in SIS circles 17000 (Cairo), was described only as '17 Land' and nothing else. His assistant would be 17200 and so on. Agents recruited by 17200 would be numbered from zero, so his first would be 201 his second 202 and so on. These would be shown in the completed code as 17201 or 17202.

Inside Micky Jourdain's Station Code Book each country has its page and in some cases the names and numbers of the Section VIII operator there. Athens is 41000 Land so we read – '41900 C. P. Meadows' and '41951 J. M. Bell'. These two members of Section VIII were very competent wireless operators but widely known just as 'Curly' and 'Dinger'.

Chapter 11 is about Edgar's service in Greece. On disembarking at Alexandria after his subsequent escape from Crete, he reports being met by Colonel Casson who said 'You must know how pleased I am to see you!'

One feels like adding – *so you should be* – after abandoning a man with so much confidential knowledge, cyphers and secret wireless gear, in their Packard near the northern frontier of Greece, with the enemy forces moving rapidly towards the area.

Edgar was told to wait for instructions but Casson already knew the dangers after reading the SIGINT messages received by wireless before leaving Edgar alone. Casson went down to Athens and departed in a flying boat – apparently waiting at Piraeus. Even then, he did not bother to send a short signal instructing Edgar to move back to Athens and away from the imminent danger of capture.

Luckily for Casson – after waiting vainly for the promised instructions – Edgar took it upon himself to leave Yannina and drove his Packard 'SLU' south to Athens but the road was bombed and strafed by German aircraft all the way. Athens was uncannily quiet and he found the Military Mission and the British Embassy abandoned. Fortunately, for everyone concerned, he bravely spent valuable time in destroying the wireless gear and cyphers in the secret wireless station he had built in his bedroom of the Grande Bretagne Hotel.

He then drove back to the courtyard of the deserted Embassy where he abandoned the Packard – after destroying all the wireless and documents in that as well.

Only after this essential work was completed did Edgar think of his own safety and start to belatedly follow the Mission and Embassy staff out of Athens. However, he did not have the benefit of an aircraft waiting and instead joined a train full of retreating troops and frightened civilians, all heading for Corinth and the south.

Casson lamely said afterwards that most of the Mission itself was just whisked off in the flying boat and 'he had no option'. But, even accepting his abandoning Edgar up at Yannina and later being – 'whisked off' – it would have only taken a thirty-second wireless message to get him started on his journey south towards Athens. That would have been away from the advancing Axis troops and the potential calamity of their capturing Edgar with his growing knowledge of the infant Ultra, his secret documents and wireless gear.

Appendix 6

The Conflict in Yugoslavia

The Balkans, and particularly Yugoslavia, have often been at the heart of world conflict – the most famous example being the assassination of Archduke Franz Ferdinand of Austria at Sarajevo in 1914 that set off World War 1. It is a diverse region of a number of ethnic and religious groups including Croatians, Muslims, Albanians, Christians (of both Catholic and Orthodox persuasions), Serbs and Slovenes. There are sub-regions within the region, both territorial and ethnic.

This was the complex political and military situation in Yugoslavia that Edgar found in 1941. It was the result of years of ethnic hatred amongst the different nationalities and religious groups making up the region. To explain this seemingly endless strife is best left to the many authors – better qualified than I – who have written about its problems. My aim here is just to give the reader an outline of the main factions Edgar faced by landing – relatively innocently – to aid a General who he thought was fighting a common enemy – the Axis partnership of Italy and Germany.

As I have said, there were many factions involved but I will concentrate on the two main ones that ensured continued upheaval amongst the peoples of this troubled region. However, before that I should say I have examined numerous books and reports on this war. I found that in addition to these major participants, the Ustasi forces of Croatia were also conducting a ghastly campaign fighting with the German and Italian forces with whom they had allied themselves.

Apologists for the various factions have tried to explain the conduct of their forces in World War II. However, the world has again seen some of the underlying hatred that exists in the region during the war in 1991 – with quite dreadful bloodshed across Bosnia and Croatia.

It is not surprising that Edgar said he was 'delighted beyond measure' when word came through by code from ISLD in Cairo, that he should leave the country. The fighting was to be expected but it was the constant fear of betrayal and deceit that concerned him most.

Mihailovic and the Chetniks

Born in Ivanjica, Kingdom of Serbia, Mihailovic went to the Serbian Military Academy in October 1910 and as a cadet fought in the Balkan Wars 1912–1913. In July 1913 he was given the rank of Second Lieutenant as the top soldier in his class. He served in World War I and together with the Serbian Army marched through Albania in 1915 during the long retreat of the Serbian Army. He later received several decorations for his achievements on the Salonica front.

Between the wars he became a Staff Officer (elite of Serbian/Yugoslav Army) and achieved the rank of Colonel. He also served as Military Attaché in Sofia and Prague.

His military career almost came to an abrupt end after several incidents, the most important one being the idea of dividing the Yugoslav Army along national lines into Serbs, Croats and Slovenes, for which he was sentenced to 30 days imprisonment. World War II found Mihailovic occupying a minor position of assistant to Chief of Staff of the Second Army.

Following the Yugoslav defeat by Germany in April 1941, a small group of officers and soldiers led by Mihailovic refused to surrender and retreated in hope of finding Yugoslav Army units still fighting in the mountains. After arriving at Ravna Gora in Serbia on May 8, he realised that his little group of seven officers plus twenty-four non-commissioned officers and soldiers was the only one.

On June 14th, Mihailovic organized the Chetnik detachment of the Yugoslav Army. These Chetnik formations led by him, later became the Military-Chetnik detachments and finally – 'The Yugoslav Army of the Homeland'. The stated goal of the Chetniks was the liberation of the country from the occupying Armies, including the forces of Nazi Germany, Fascist Italy and the Ustasi (the fascist regime of Croatia).

The British Special Operations Executive was being sent to aid Mihailovic's forces beginning with the autumn of 1941. Mihailovic rose in rank and stature, becoming the Minister of War of the Government in Exile in January 11, 1942 and General and Deputy Commander-in-Chief on June 17 the same year.

The Chetniks were forced to move to eastern Bosnia where they engaged in heavy combat with the Ustasi, resulting in

General Draza Mihailovic, leader of the Chetnik army that eventually called itself the 'Yugoslav Army of the Homeland'.

several incidents of war crimes against people who supported the other faction. It is unclear however, how much say Mihailovic himself had in these incidents.

The movement was highly decentralized, and in that way was more like a collective of many small regional guerrilla groups that shared the same name, rather than a unified Army under complete control of Mihailovic and his staff.

In 1943, the Germans decided to pursue the Chetniks in the northern zone, and offered a reward of 100,000 Reichsmarks for the capture of Mihailovic, dead or alive.

By the middle of 1943, the Partisan movement under Tito had successfully survived an intense period of Axis pressure, while the Chetniks had almost entirely abandoned anti-fascist activities in favour of fighting the Partisans. Consequently, at the Teheran Conference in November 1943, a decision was made by the Allies to cease their support of the Chetniks, and switch allegiance to Tito's Partisans who were the main anti-fascist resistance group in Yugoslavia.

Towards the end of the war, Mihailovic went into hiding in East Bosnia. Nikola Kalabic, his comrade from the war was the only person who knew where Mihailovic had taken refuge. In exchange for his freedom, since Kalabic was wanted as well, he revealed where Draza Mihailovic was hiding.

Mihailovic was captured by the Partisans on 13th March 1946. Convicted of collaborating with the enemy, he was executed on 17th July 1946. In spite of the many accusations levelled at Mihailovic and the Chetniks, one aspect of his campaign led to his being awarded the Legion of Merit by President Truman.

The Legion of Merit

Due to the efforts of Major Richard L. Felman and his friends, President Harry S. Truman, on the recommendation of General Dwight D. Eisenhower, posthumously awarded Mihailovic the Legion of Merit in 1948 for the rescue of American Airmen by Chetniks. For the first time in history, this high award and the story of the rescue was classified secret by the State Department so as not to offend the communist government of Yugoslavia.

Mihailovic near the end of the war. He was captured by the Partisans, tried then shot by firing squad in 1946.

"General Dragoljub Mihailovich distinguished himself in an outstanding manner as Commander-in-Chief of the Yugoslavian Army Forces and later as Minister of War by organizing and leading important resistance forces against the enemy which occupied Yugoslavia, from December 1941 to December 1944. Through the undaunted efforts of his troops, many United States airmen were rescued and returned safely to friendly control. General Mihailovic and his forces, although lacking adequate supplies, and fighting under extreme hardships, contributed materially to the Allied cause, and were instrumental in obtaining a final Allied victory."

Signed March 29th, 1948, Harry S. Truman.

It was sixty years after the rescue of the American airmen, on May 9th, 2005, that General Mihailovic's daughter Gordana was finally presented with the decoration bestowed posthumously on her father by President Truman in 1948. The ceremony was a private one without any publicity.

The Legion of Merit awarded posthumously to Draza Mihailovic by President Harry Truman on the advice of General Eisenhower but not actually presented to his family until 2005.

Josip Broz 'Tito' and the Partisans

Josip Broz was born in 1892 in Croatia, then part of Austria-Hungary. He was the seventh child of Franjo and Marija Broz. His father, Franjo Broz, was a Croat, while his mother Marija was a Slovene.

In 1920 he joined the Communist Party of Yugoslavia (CPY) and its influence on the political life of the Kingdom of Yugoslavia was growing rapidly. In the 1920 elections the Communists won 59 seats and became the third strongest party. The King's regime would not tolerate the CPY and declared it illegal. In 1921 all Communist-won mandates were nullified. Broz continued his work underground despite pressure on Communists from the government.

Having adopted the code-name 'Tito' he travelled to the Soviet Union in 1935, working for a year in the Balkan section of the Comintern. He was a member of the Soviet Communist Party and the Soviet secret police (NKVD). In 1936, the Comintern sent him back to Yugoslavia to purge the Communist Party there. In 1937, Stalin had the Secretary-General of the CPY Milan Gorkic murdered in Moscow. The same year, Tito returned again from the Soviet Union to Yugoslavia after being named there by Stalin as Secretary-General of the still-outlawed CPY. During this period, he faithfully followed

Comintern policy, criticizing Fascist Italy and Nazi Germany until the pact of 1939, and then switching to a criticism of western democracies until 1941.

On April 6th, 1941, German, Italian and Hungarian forces attacked Yugoslavia. The Luftwaffe bombed Belgrade and other major Yugoslav cities. On April 17th, representatives of Yugoslavia's legitimate government and the military signed an armistice with Germany at Belgrade, ending eleven days of resistance against the invading German Wehrmacht.

The Independent State of Croatia was established as a Nazi puppet-state, ruled by the Ustasi the militant wing of the Croatian Party of Rights, from which it split off in 1929. Until 1941, it was in exile in Italy, and was therefore limited in its activities. German troops occupied Bosnia and Herzegovina as well as part of Serbia and Slovenia, while other parts of the country were occupied by Bulgaria, Hungary and Italy.

Tito and his leading staff during the 'Yugoslav People's Liberation War'. Left to right: Alexsander Rancovic, Marshal of Yugoslavia Josip Broz Tito, and Milovan Dilas.

Tito did not initially respond to the German invasion because of Stalin's non-aggression pact with Nazi Germany. After Germany attacked the Soviet Union on June 22nd, 1941, Tito called a Central Committee meeting on July 4th, 1941, which named him Military Commander and issued a call to Arms.

The Partisans soon began a widespread and successful guerrilla campaign and started liberating chunks of territory and was one of the early anti-fascist units in Europe. Their growing and successful activities provoked the Germans into "retaliation" against civilians that resulted in mass murders. For each German soldier killed, 100 civilians were to be killed and 50 for each wounded.

In the areas 'liberated' by the Partisans they organized people's committees to act as civilian government. In 1943 Tito was named President of the National Committee of Liberation and on December 4, 1943, while most of the country was still occupied by the Axis – Tito proclaimed a provisional democratic Yugoslav government.

Tito's Partisans faced competition from the largely Serbian Chetniks, who had long been supported by the British and the Royal government in exile. After the Partisans stood up to intense Axis attacks between January and June 1943, Allied leaders switched their support to them. There is no doubt that much 'lobbying' was done on Tito's behalf and the factional war conducted by Chetniks was detrimental to the Mihailovic cause. The British SOE (Special Operations Executive) in Yugoslavia put their weight behind Tito's forces and so ended the direct support for Mihailovic.

President Roosevelt, Winston Churchill and Joseph Stalin officially recognised the Partisans at the Teheran Conference. This resulted in substantial Allied aid being parachuted behind Axis lines to assist them. The Partisans were supported directly by Allied airdrops to their headquarters, with Brigadier Fitzroy Maclean of SOE playing a significant role in the liaison missions. However, due to his close ties to Stalin, Tito often quarrelled with the British and American Staff Officers attached to his headquarters.

In the meantime, the forces loyal to Mihailovic continued their struggle against the occupying forces and the Partisans, without military supplies or support of any kind from the British and Allied powers.

Sadly, this racial and religious motivated inter-Yugoslavian warfare cost hundreds of thousands of lives of people of the region. Estimates vary between 400,000 and 700,000 – totally unconnected with the war against the Axis powers occupying their troubled land.

The Ustasi forces of Croatia

Having mentioned the Partisans and Chetniks it would be remiss not to mention the Ustasi in a little more detail. When it was founded in 1929, the Ustasi was a nationalist organization that sought to create an Independent Croatian state. Hitler put the Ustasi into power in this deeply Catholic country following his conquest of Yugoslavia. Its military wing then became the Ustasi Army.

With occupation by the Axis forces Ustasi bands roamed the country and killed Jews and Serbs with unbelievable cruelty. There are many detailed reports describing the Ustasi horror then perpetrated on the people including rape, maiming, torture, burning. However, I have decided not to repeat details of them in this book. That bands of Ustasi behaved in a most inhuman and depraved manner, seemingly without censure from the Croatian government, is substantiated by the fact that even the Germans and Italians baulked and complained at the depth of depravity of its members.

Appendix 7

Appointments in MI6 Section VIII

Unless you were a member of Section VIII yourself, you might question how Edgar Harrison – a regular soldier 'recruited' into MI6 – could be a sergeant one day, and then appear as a commissioned officer ready to be parachuted into Yugoslavia the next.

John Darwin gives an indication of the 'flexibility' of the Section VIII military rules in the extraordinary diary he kept during the years 1938 to 1940. (See my book 'The Secret Wireless War' – Chapter 21). Darwin was a friend and confidant of Admiral Sir Hugh Sinclair Head of SIS – until his death on 4th November 1939. On 15th November 1939 Darwin records in his diary *'Jordain had a successful trip to Royal Corps of Signals at Reading. We can apparently get people in and out of the army as we please. A most satisfactory proceeding!'*

I added, *'This prepared the ground for the later militarisation of the unit, seemingly as a real part of the Royal Corps of Signals.'* The 'Jourdain' mentioned was Lt. Col. Jourdain. At that time he was considered likely to become the deputy to Richard Gambier-Parry Head of Section VIII. If the unit could get a man into or out of the Army at will, it was certainly no problem to alter his rank to suit a particular situation arising. It was clearly possible to appoint signalmen to be NCOs (non-commissioned officers) as well as commissioned officers – if needed.

The first of the '**N**ot **P**aid **A**rmy **F**unds' (NPAF) personnel appeared in the routine 'Daily Orders' that was started at Whaddon Hall as a further part of the plan to disguise Section VIII's function, under the appearance of an army unit. Later on, they were referred to in the unit's Daily Orders just as – 'Special Enlistments' – in what were otherwise strictly military-looking 'Daily Orders'.

Those 'Not Paid Army Funds' were given the standard Army Pay Book (known as 'AB 64 Part 1) which was proof of identity, a record of service, listed training, inoculations and contained names of relatives and one's last will and testament. Most of the Section VIII 'enlistments' into the Army and certainly those who had to travel to other units –

had an insert in the book marked 'This man is on special duty and has permission to wear civilian clothes.'

All 'real' Army personnel had another section called an AB64 Part 2, and this actually showed the owner's pay rates and pay received. None of the Section VIII personnel was issued with AB64 Part 2.

Many of the staff working 'inside' Whaddon were Special Enlistments and they would wear civilian clothes whenever possible. Sports jackets and flannels were fairly common amongst the Section VIII personnel when off duty. It seems extraordinary looking back that we had such a relaxed approach at times, whilst so very deeply committed to the war effort.

This then, is the world that Edgar Harrison entered in January 1940, after over ten years of a strictly military upbringing. He now found himself a member of Section VIII, paid by MI6 and not the army. I venture to suggest the seeming laissez-faire attitude came as a shock to him, as it did to the others who joined Section VIII from a normal military background.

I will give my own knowledge of 'Special Enlistments' – 'Not Paid Army Funds' – 'Army Ranks' – 'Wearing civilian clothes' – as well as information from others involved.

Special Enlistments and Not Paid Army Funds
All personnel of MI6 Section VIII became members of the Royal Corps of Signals. I am fortunate in still having details of my own special enlistment as shown on Part 1 orders dated 9th December 1943.

Part 2 Orders dated 6th December 1943, shows the expression 'Not paid army funds' against my name and others further down the page. This was sometimes shortened to NPAF.

Opposite: Daily Orders of Special Communication Unit No. 1. (SCU)
dated 9th December 1943 and Geoffrey Pidgeon is listed as a
'Special Enlistment' in the section at the bottom of the page.

DAILY ORDERS PART I
BY
LIEUT-COL. G. ROOKER, R. SIGNALS
COMMANDING, SPECIAL COMMUNICATIONS UNIT NO. 1.

Issue No. 292.   9 Dec 43.

1576. DUTIES AND ROUTINE.

	10 Dec 43	11 Dec 43
Duty Officer of the Day	To be detailed by No.7 SCU	Lieut. H.J. Castleman
Duty Warrant Officer	RSM. V.W. Robinson	CQMS. J.F. Brash
Orderly Sergeant	Corpl.N. Sutherland	To be detailed by No.7 SCU
Camp Piquet	Lo.Corpl. C.F. Anderson	Lo. L/Cpl. A.G. Dudley
	Sigmn. J.H. Cook and	Sigmn. E.H. Tyler and
	2 men to be detailed by	2 men to be detailed by
	No. 7 SCU.	No. 7 SCU.

Night Fire Piquet -   Period 13 Dec 43 to 19 Dec 43.
N.C.O. i/c to be detailed by Depot Group.
M.T. Group and Depot Group will each detail two men.
Two men to be detailed by No.7 SCU.

Reveille	0630	1st Works Parade 0900	Tea	1715-1800
Check Parade	0655	Dinner	1200-1215	Piquet Mounting 1800
Breakfast	0645-0800	Dinner	1230-1315	Tattoo	2200
Sick Parade	0815	2nd Works Parade 1355	Roll Call	2230
P.T. & Drill 0830-0900	Tea	1630-1645	Lights Out	2245

Black-out times for 9 Dec 43 are from 1721 to 0824.

1577. BARRACK INSPECTION.
There will be a barrack inspection, (including Canteen, Cookhouse, Sergeants
Mess and Tailor's Shop) at noon on Saturday, 11 Dec 43.

1578. POSTING - INTERNAL.
2344513 Serjt. (Loc. CQMS.) G. Laidler
is posted from Depot Group to No. 1 Special Operations Group w.e.f. 10 Dec 43.

1579. COMPULSORY EVACUATION OF HOMES IN S.W. ENGLAND.
Personnel whose families are being compelled to evacuate from S.W. England
are entitled to compassionate leave with a free railway warrant in addition
to normal leave and free warrant entitlement.   In cases where personnel have
paid their own fares refunds may be claimed at military rates.
Officers are entitled to additional free warrants for the above purpose
up to and including the rank of Captain.

1580. AFRICA STAR RIBBON, EMBLEM AND CLASP.
All personnel who claim to hold the necessary qualifications to enable them
to receive the Africa Star will hand in their number, rank, name and initials -
Officers to the Adjutant and O.Rs. to the Orderly Room - not later than noon
on Friday 10 Dec 43.   This is in addition to their official application on
AFB.2063.
Part I Order No. 1542 dated 2 Dec 43 refers.

1581. CANCELLATION - COURT OF INQUIRY.
Part I Order No. 1545 dated 2 Dec 43 is cancelled.

1582. ENLISTMENTS - O.Rs.
2602899 Sigmn. S.H. Cole
specially enlisted in this Unit on 26 Nov 43 and is posted to No.1 Operations
Group w.e.f. same date.
N.Y.A. Rct. G. Pidgeon
specially enlisted in this Unit on 30 Nov 43 and is posted to No.2 Technical
Group w.e.f. same date.

1583. DISCIPLINE - OUT OF BOUNDS.
No. 7 S.C.U. Lines are out of bounds to all O.Rs. of No. 1 S.C.U. except
when on duty.

To Sheet Two.............

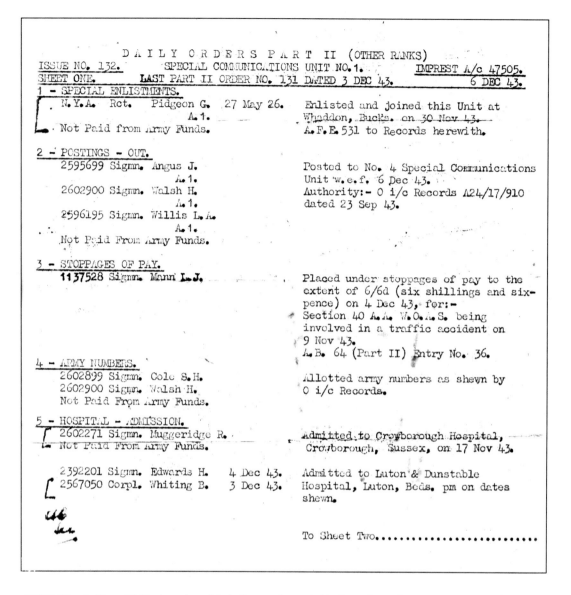

DAILY ORDERS PART II (OTHER RANKS)
ISSUE NO. 132.   SPECIAL COMMUNICATIONS UNIT NO. 1.   IMPREST A/c 47505.
SHEET ONE.   LAST PART II ORDER NO. 131 DATED 3 DEC 43.   6 DEC 43.

1 - SPECIAL ENLISTMENTS.
     N.Y.A.   Rct.   Pidgeon G.   27 May 26.   Enlisted and joined this Unit at
           A. 1.   Whaddon, Bucks. on 30 Nov 43.
     Not Paid from Army Funds.   A.F.E. 531 to Records herewith.

2 - POSTINGS - OUT.
     2595699 Sigmn. Angus J.   Posted to No. 4 Special Communications
           A. 1.   Unit w.e.f. 6 Dec 43.
     2602900 Sigmn. Walsh H.   Authority:- O i/c Records A24/17/910
           A. 1.   dated 23 Sep 43.
     2596195 Sigmn. Willis L.A.
           A. 1.
     Not Paid From Army Funds.

3 - STOPPAGES OF PAY.
     1137528 Sigmn. Mann L.J.   Placed under stoppages of pay to the
                                         extent of 6/6d (six shillings and six-
                                         pence) on 4 Dec 43, for:-
                                         Section 40 A.A. W.O.A.S. being
                                         involved in a traffic accident on
                                         9 Nov 43.
                                         A.B. 64 (Part II) Entry No. 36.

4 - ARMY NUMBERS.
     2602899 Sigmn. Cole S.H.   Allotted army numbers as shewn by
     2602900 Sigmn. Walsh H.   O i/c Records.
     Not Paid From Army Funds.

5 - HOSPITAL - ADMISSION.
     2602271 Sigmn. Muggeridge R.   Admitted to Crowborough Hospital,
     Not Paid From Army Funds.   Crowborough, Sussex, on 17 Nov 43.

     2392201 Sigmn. Edwards H.   4 Dec 43.   Admitted to Luton & Dunstable
     2567050 Corpl. Whiting B.   3 Dec 43.   Hospital, Luton, Beds. pm on dates
                                           shewn.

                                         To Sheet Two.........................

SCU No, 1. Part II Orders dated 9th December 1943 describing (RCT: recruit) Pidgeon G. as having enlisted but "Not Paid Army Funds." In other words, like others in the unit, I was paid by MI6 Section VIII.

Wearing civilian clothes as required

Many of us had a note inserted into our Part 1 Pay Book (AB64 Part 1), to the effect that we were on special duty and entitled to wear civilian clothes.

I no longer have my own AB64 Part 1 Pay Book but the illustration is that from my father's. I should mention that he was a member of Section VIII and in charge of the SCU wireless stores at Whaddon Hall.

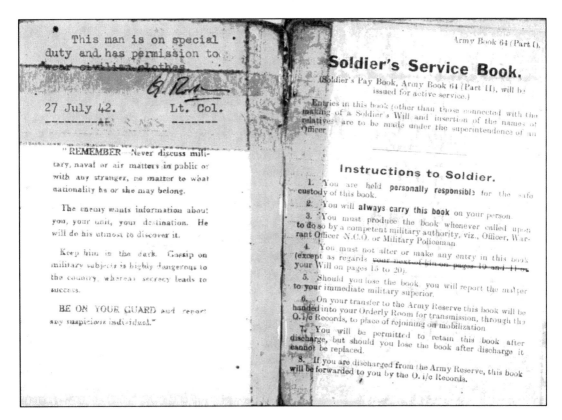

A slip added to our pay books – showing the bearer being on special duty and authorised to civilian clothes. This one is from my father's Part 1 Pay Book – AB64.

Army ranks

All the non-commissioned ranks in Section VIII were 'Local'. That is to say they would not apply in the highly unlikely event that one had to join another unit. My father, for example, was a WO2 (Warrant Officer Class 2) and quite appropriate for his role in charge of our wireless stores. However, in his discharge papers, in spite of that somewhat grandiose title, he is listed just as a 'Signalman (Local WO2)' and a Signalman is the equivalent of a Private soldier.

Those necessarily appointed as Officers, i.e. Lieutenant and upwards, were mostly Territorial Commissions and sometimes a Lord Lieutenant's Commission. Clearly, they are more easily appointed than those holding a King's Commission.

The advantage was that these ranks were given as required by the situation, quite unlike other military units. One more thing set us even further apart. Wilf Lilburn and Tommy Ord on occasions wore RAF uniform and I believe Wilf Lilburn also wore that of a Naval Officer – if the situation required. My boss Dennis Smith for example, also wore RAF uniform for a time. However, when army attire or one's 'rank' was inappropriate you could easily – and legally – change into civilian clothes and you carried the necessary papers that showed you could not be challenged by military or civil authority.

Nevertheless, Edgar could hardly have travelled to war torn Yugoslavia in his civilian clothes!

There are many examples of unusual promotions in other secret units. One such was Henry Dryden, a civilian member of GC&CS at Bletchley Park. Whilst in France in 1940, and with the German Blitzkrieg just underway, Dryden was given an emergency commission in the field by General Mason-Macfarlane, the Director of Military Intelligence. Dryden later reports in 'Code Breakers' that just prior to the Battle of El Alamein "…I was in quick succession promoted to the rank of Major….".

During the war there were many promotions of a 'Temporary' nature in the regular army unconnected with our unit. For example, I know of a Major in the Royal Signals promoted to 'War Substantive' Lt. Col. in May 1944 *and in the same month* listed as a 'Temporary Colonel' *and in the same month* he is later listed as 'Temporary Brigadier'. In 1946 he reverted to Lt. Col.

A number of SOE officers sent to work in occupied Crete and the Balkans were rapidly advanced in rank. Some were promoted to Major and one to Lt. Colonel. According to Antony Beevor – *"..This rank inflation was intended mainly to give them weight when dealing with local guerrilla groups…"*. How similar this report is to Edgar appearing before General Mihailovic as a Lieutenant instead of as a Sergeant!

Civilians – men and women alike – recruited into SOE in Britain would, on completion of their training, frequently find themselves 'instantly' an officer in one of the services. I mean absolutely no criticism of these SOE promotions but they merely point to the 'flexibility' that clearly existed in other secret units – outside of MI6.

Appendix 8

The 'Way' Mission and
Edgar Harrison's role in Russia

One of my most difficult problems in sorting through Edgar's drafts concerns the reason for his visit to Russia. On the face of it, he was included in the Way Mission to provide them with wireless communications to Cairo and London and to install wireless equipment in the 'armoured vehicles' being delivered to Russia by the southern route. But, there had to be a third reason.

At that time, there must have been hundreds of army wireless mechanics in the armoured divisions in North Africa. Certainly – however limited and basic their training – they were perfectly capable of assembling and fitting standard army wireless sets in tanks. Bear in mind, hundreds of tanks from Britain and particularly the United States had been delivered to the 8th Army zone in North Africa. No doubt all had to have their wireless sets fitted on arrival. Here we have Edgar Harrison, one of the finest wireless operators in the Middle East at the time, surely wasted on carrying out such a relatively mundane task.

I have tried to find out the answer to this riddle through the good offices of MI6 at Vauxhall Bridge Cross but they cannot suggest a reason. It is clear he had the important job of providing secure communications for the Mission to London and Kuybeshev. However, why risk sending a man of his skills and growing importance near the front to install wireless sets into tanks – where he and his Russian crews eventually came under constant fire?

As mentioned earlier, the fact is that he accompanied John Bruce Lockhart from Cairo separately from the main 'Way Mission' team and joined them at Habaniyah. We know that Bruce Lockhart was also now a member of ISLD (SIS) and so we have two ISLD members in a Mission, ostensibly just about supplies, the administration of supplies and in the case of Edgar, fitting standard army wireless sets in tanks, and providing communications to London and Cairo.

It seems likely that Edgar's work on the armoured vehicles was a cover for reporting intelligence gleaned by the team and monitored by John Bruce Lockhart – in addition to providing their top-level communications. After all, the 'Way Mission' was one of the few British units in World War II with any level of freedom to move amongst the Russian forces.

We should also take note that the leader of the Mission, Colonel Way, was a Colonel in the Royal Artillery – but also happened to be Deputy Director of Military Intelligence at GHQ Middle East Command!

Given that such an important part of the Mission was intelligence personnel, then intelligence gathering was probably the major role for them – with the fitting of armoured vehicles a convenient cover. If that was the case, then using Edgar's exceptional skills in wireless communications – supposedly to fit the wireless sets into tanks – begins to make sense.

However, whatever benefits arose from the Mission's intelligence gathering – it was risky to allow it to develop to the point that Edgar became involved on the battlefield itself.

Appendix 9

LRDG – The Long Range Desert Group

In World War One, the fighting in the Western Desert led to the formation of a small unit called the Light Car Patrol. This unit used Ford Model T cars to get around in the desert. At the end of hostilities the unit was disbanded and their records were stored, for surely nothing like them would ever be needed again.

Between the wars there was a group of British Officers that relished the thought of going around in the desert in motor vehicles. One of these officers was Major Ralph Bagnold (1896-1990) who was the son of a British Army Royal Engineer. He followed the family tradition and in 1915 became an officer in the Royal Engineers during World War I after training at Woolwich. His speciality was communications and he joined the Royal Engineers Signal Service. After spending three years of active duty in France, he took leave to study engineering at Cambridge University, graduating with honours and then returned to service.

A Royal Warrant for the creation of a Corps of Signals was signed by the then Secretary of State for War, Winston Churchill, on 28th June 1920. Six weeks later, King George V conferred the title Royal Corps of Signals.

During the interim war years Bagnold was stationed in Cairo and while on leave began exploring the desert in personal vehicles, with his friends and later LRDG associates including, Capt. Patrick Clayton, Capt. William B. Kennedy Shaw and Major Guy Prendergast.

Major Ralph Bagnold who devised and formed the Long Range Desert Group.

In 1934 Bagnold was discharged at the rank of Major with a permanent disability. This however did not stop him from his scientific investigation of the 'Physics of Blown Sand'. And in early 1938 he participated in one final trip into the Egyptian desert.

At the onset of hostilities in 1939, Major Bagnold was again called up to service in the Signals. On his way to his post in East Africa, the ship he was on was involved in an accident in the Mediterranean and had to put into Port Said for repairs. While awaiting the repairs to be completed, he made a trip into Cairo to visit some of his old friends. It was there that he was summoned to the office of General Wavell.

After a short conversation with the General, they both decided that he could best serve his country in Egypt. During his early days in Egypt he submitted (on two separate occasions) to his superiors, plans for the formation of a Light Car Patrol Unit. His request and suggestions were denied.

Then in June of 1940 the Italians attacked Egypt. He submitted his third and last copy that had been written six months earlier. This time it was noticed and brought to the attention of General Wavell. He was in the General's office within the hour. After explaining his ideas in detail, basically reconnaissance and intelligence gathering along with a little 'High-sea-piracy!' General Wavell approved the plan. He gave him six weeks to be ready and gave him a letter that stated:

> 'To all Heads of Departments and Branches.
> I wish any request by Major Bagnold in person to be granted
> immediately and without question.'

With this in hand he went about the arduous task of getting his unit operational within the six weeks allotted. He rounded up some of his old desert travelling companions (Captains Pat Clayton & Wm. Shaw). Wm. Kennedy Shaw was to train the men in desert navigation and for that training they set up a series of supply dumps across the desert.

Formation and Equipment

The unit, initially known as the Long Range Patrols, was founded on 3rd July 1940 and 150 New Zealand volunteers were selected with the permission of General Freyberg, the New Zealand Commanding General in the Middle East theatre. Bagnold had reasoned that the New Zealanders, being mostly farmers, would be more adept at using and maintaining machinery. Later additions to the group included British, Rhodesian and Indian units.

The unit was arranged into 3 main patrols, of 40 soldiers each. Patrols were initially equipped with his chosen vehicles that were quickly modified to his specifications – Ford F30 4WD and Chevrolet WB trucks, supported by Chevrolet 1311x1 – 15 cwt (3/4 ton) command cars. The patrol trucks were later replaced with Chevrolet 1533x2 -- 30 cwt (1.5 ton) trucks, and the command cars with Willys Jeeps.

Two of the patrol vehicles used by the LRDG but only after considerable amendments had taken place to suit the arduous work they were called upon to perform.

Each patrol was equipped with ten Lewis machine guns, four Boys anti-tank rifles, and a Bofors 37 mm anti-tank gun; later on, trucks were equipped with Browning .50 cal machine guns, captured Italian Breda 20 mm anti-aircraft guns and twin mounted .303 cal Vickers K machine guns. The troops carried Thompson submachine guns, and other standard British infantry weapons.

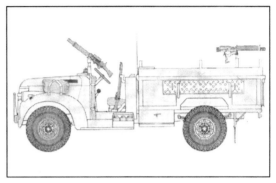

The primary wireless set of the patrols was the British Army No. 11 wireless set using the end-fed Wyndom aerial for long-range communications of up to 1,200 miles.

A drawing of a LRDG Patrol vehicle by Tobias Gibson. This is a Lewis machine gun fitted near the windscreen, a Lee Enfield rifle beside the driver and a Vickers machine gun near the tail.

Initial Training
During the initial training, Shaw continued teaching navigation, whilst Bagnold taught communications.

Combat History
On 13th September 1940, the unit formed its first base at the Siwa Oasis. They arrived there by driving approximately 240 km across the Egyptian Sand Sea. On 15th September two patrols of the LRDG were engaged in the unit's first combat operations. In this action Captain Mitford's unit travelled via the Kalansho Sand Sea and attacked Italian petrol dumps and emergency landing fields along the Palificata. Meanwhile, Clayton's group

After the defeat of the Italians – General Erwin Rommel and his Afrika Corps became the main adversary of Bagnold and the LRDG.

passed through Italian territory to contact the French forces in Chad. The patrols joined at the southern tip of the Gilf Kebir (where a supply dump was located) and then returned to Cairo, via the Kharga Oasis. Each patrol had travelled approximately 6,000km.

Following the September expedition, the War Office realised the patrols were so successful that in December of 1940, the personnel was doubled in size to 350 men. At the same time, the size of the Patrols was cut from 10 trucks to 5 trucks and the number of patrols doubled. Coinciding with this, the unit was renamed the Long Range Desert Group (LRDG). Bagnold was promoted to Lieutenant-Colonel. The enlarged unit gathered volunteers from British, Indian, and Rhodesian units.

Bagnold wrote: *'During the next few months, raids were made on a number of enemy-held oases …isolated garrisons were shot up…our raiders seemed to the Italians to appear from a fourth dimension…Graziani [the Italian Commander-in-Chief], was beginning to doubt his intelligence reports [and] the Italian army halted for months.'*

Chad and Kufra

In September 1940, Bagnold travelled to Fort Lamy in Chad, where he helped persuade the French colony to join the Allies. The LRDG and Free French forces worked together to raid Italian positions in the area of the Murzuk Oasis and the combined forces, using French artillery, captured Kufra. In April 1941, the LRDG's headquarters was moved to Kufra.

Bagnold wrote: *'Temperatures exceeding 50°C were found to be tolerable, even on a restricted water ration, owing to the dryness. The worst discomfort came from sandstorms, which lasted several days. They made eating very difficult.'*

From Kufra, the LRDG Commanders would essentially serve as the military commanders of a region approximately the size of northern Europe, a region that had not seen rain in 70 years.

Bagnold leaves the LRDG and Prendergast takes over. During the summer of 1941, Bagnold had recruited another of his prewar exploration companions, Guy Lennox Prendergast to serve as his second-in-command. On 1st July Bagnold left the unit, to serve in Cairo as a full Colonel, and Prendergast became the LRDG's Commander. During the unit's short history in North Africa (September 1940 until May 1943), there was only one week that it did not have active patrols behind the enemy lines.

Link with SAS

The SAS was raised by then Lieutenant Archibald David Stirling a Supplementary Reserve Officer of the Scots Guards during World War II as 'L' Detachment, SAS Brigade, (so named from August 24th, 1941) adding to the pre-existing 'J' and 'K' Detachments of the notional Special Air Service Brigade. Given the acting rank of Captain by the Commander in Chief, Middle East Forces and an initial authorised strength of 68 all ranks, Stirling's No 1 Special Service Unit was originally created as an all-volunteer airborne force to conduct raids and sabotage far behind enemy lines in the desert on the model of a concept worked out by Lieutenant John Steel Lewes.

Lewes, an experienced weapons training instructor with the Welsh Guards prior to service with No 8 Commando, became the Detachment's first Chief Instructor. 'L' Detachment operated in conjunction with the Long Range Desert Group (LRDG) now commanded by Lieutenant-Colonel Guy Lennox Prendergast who later became Deputy Commander of the SAS Brigade in North West Europe in 1944.

Driver in an LRDG vehicle with a Lee Enfield rifle to his side.

Other operations

After the end of the African campaign, the LRDG was trained in mountain warfare at the Cedars of Lebanon Hotel, in Lebanon. They were also trained in parachute operations. The unit went on to serve in the Greek islands, Italy and in Normandy.

Edgar at Kufra

It was to the Kufra Oasis – headquarters of the Long Range Desert Group – that Edgar Harrison brought the ISLD (MI6

LRDG patrols in the desert illustrating the amount of equipment they had to carry in covering such tremendous distances in hostile country.

– SIS), agents' wireless station and training camp in 1942. He and his men had to rapidly become acclimatised to the heat, the rugged terrain and vast desolation of the desert.

He tells us of his work in the desert and of his unit's part in saving men from the ill-fated SAS raid on Benghazi.

Appendix 10

SCUs in the campaign in Sicily and Italy

By this time in World War II the role of Ultra was very significant. From the early dark days of Crete the knowledge given by the Codebreakers at Bletchley Park had empowered our service Commanders from Admiral Cunningham defeating the Italians at Matapan, through the North African campaign until this point. Of course, as in Crete, it was one thing to know what the threat was, and where it was coming from, but something quite different to take the appropriate steps. Shortage of men and material still precluded using the information to our advantage. However, the SIGINT provided, had allowed the RAF to substantially reduce German supplies from Europe crossing the Mediterranean to supply Rommel. And, with their growing military strength, Allied Commanders were able to more fully utilize the intelligence provided by Ultra.

A number of SLUs had been built up in North Africa after the 'Torch' invasion led by General Eisenhower and so prepared the Allied forces for the return to Europe. The first step was the invasion of Sicily and was a major Allied amphibious and airborne operation involving American, British, and Canadian forces, tasked with taking the island from the Axis forces of Italy and Germany.

A major part of the planning for the invasion was based on Ultra information being supplied to General Eisenhower and his staff. This meant that the SLU stations created at Algiers and elsewhere were extremely busy. One of the operators in Algiers handling the Ultra traffic was Ray Small who later became a colleague of mine at SCU11/12 in Calcutta in1945.

He had been in Algiers at our 'Station Sybil' located on the 6th floor of the King George V Hotel with the SLU office right next door. They had a MkIII transmitter, an HRO receiver and with the aerials on the roof of the hotel, the service to and from Whaddon was excellent. The 'set up' is very reminiscent of Edgar's earlier wireless station on The Grande Bretagne Hotel in Athens.

Ray Small later moved the station forward to Tunis where the SCU/SLU was attached to Air-Marshal Tedder's Desert Air Force. In his diary in my possession, he tells of being on night shift some time later when the station handled a huge amount of traffic from Windy Ridge, including one classified ZZZZZ (5 Z's) denoting an Ultra message of the utmost importance. He believes it was Bletchley Park's earliest knowledge that the Italian Fleet was about to surrender.

To the great volume of Ultra military traffic being handled one should add that Winston Churchill was increasingly using the secure (and faster) lines provided by the SLU organisation, in preference to the normal channels. As we have seen, Edgar had earlier provided that service for Churchill – right into a Conference arena.

Returning to the invasion, General Dwight Eisenhower was in overall command, with General Sir Harold Alexander as Commander of land forces. The land forces were designated the Fifteenth Army Group, and comprised the British 8th Army (including the 1st Canadian Infantry Division), under General Bernard Montgomery. The U.S. 7th Army under General George S. Patton, was tasked to land at Gela, whilst the British 8th Army were to make separate landings at Pachino.

Each Army had two Corps under command. Defending the island was the Italian 6th Army made up of two Italian Corps (XII and XVI) of coastal defence units plus four front line divisions and miscellaneous units under Army Command together with the XIV German Panzerkorps.

At the Casablanca Conference held in January 1943 it was decided that a successful cross-Channel invasion of France would be impossible that year. It was agreed to use troops from the recently won North African Campaign to invade the Italian island of Sicily. The strategic goals were to remove the island as a base for Axis shipping and aircraft, allowing free passage to Allied ships in the Mediterranean Sea, and to put pressure on

General Harold Alexander appointed by General Eisenhower to be in overall charge of the invasion of Sicily.

Far left: General George S. Patton commanding the US forces in Sicily.

General Bernard Montgomery commanding the British and Canadian forces in Sicily.

the regime of Benito Mussolini in the hope of eventually having Italy struck from the war.

The attempt to knock Italy out of the war was partially successful, especially after Allied aircraft bombed the large railroad marshalling yards of Rome. However, the campaign could also act as a precursor to the invasion of Italy, although this was not actually agreed by the Allies at the time of the invasion. The Americans in particular were resisting any commitment to an operation that might conceivably delay the Normandy landings, or divert Allied power from the main theatre – France.

Canadian troops in Sicily.

The Canadian 1st Infantry was included at the insistence of Canadian Military Headquarters in the UK, a request granted by the British, displacing the veteran British 3rd Infantry Division. The change was not finalized until April 27th, when 1st Canadian Army Commander, General McNaughton, deemed Operation Husky to be a viable military undertaking and agreed to the detachment of both 1st Canadian Infantry Division and 1st Canadian Tank Brigade both of which had arrived in the United Kingdom.

The Axis defenders comprised around 365,000 Italian and around 40,000 German troops, with at least 47 tanks and about 200 artillery pieces, under the overall command of Italian General Alfredo Guzzoni.

The landings took place in extremely strong wind, which made the landings difficult but also ensured the element of surprise. Landings were made on the southern and eastern coasts of the island, with the British forces in the East and the Americans towards the West.

Four airborne drops were carried out just after midnight on the night of the 9th July - 10th July, as part of the invasion, two British, two American. The American paratroopers consisted largely of the 504th Parachute Infantry Regiment of the 82nd Airborne, making their first combat drop. The strong winds blew dropping aircraft off course and scattered them widely; the result was around half the U.S. paratroopers failed to reach their rallying points.

British glider-landed troops fared little better; only 1 out of 12 gliders landing on target, many crashing at sea. Nevertheless, the scattered airborne troops maximized their opportunities, attacking patrols and creating confusion wherever possible.

The sea landings, commenced some three hours after the airborne drops, despite the weather and met little opposition, as Italian units stationed on the shoreline lacked equipment and transport. This was fortunate because, as a result of the adverse weather, many troops landed in the wrong place, wrong order and as much as six hours behind schedule. The British walked into the port of Syracuse virtually unopposed. There, SCU operators quickly established a wireless station as an SLU to provide our Commanders with Ultra traffic right into the combat zone. Other operators worked the ISLD traffic to agents and that was the particular concern of Edgar Harrison after he joined the station.

The plans for the post-invasion battle had not been worked out; the Army Group Commander, Alexander, had not developed an operational plan. This left each Army to fight its own campaign with little coordination. Boundaries between the two armies were fixed, as was normal procedure. In the first two days progress was excellent, capturing Vizzini in the west and Augusta in the east.

Then resistance in the British sector stiffened. Montgomery persuaded Alexander to shift the inter-Army boundaries so the British could by-pass resistance and retain the key role of capturing Messina, while the Americans were given the role of protecting and supporting their flank. Historian Carlo D'Este has called this the worst strategic blunder of the campaign. It necessitated having the U.S. 45th Infantry Division break contact, move back to the beaches at Gela and thence northwest, and allowed the German XIVth Panzer Corps to escape likely encirclement. This episode was the origin of what would become greater conflicts between Montgomery and the II Corps Commander, Omar Bradley. Patton, however, did not contest the decision.

After a week's fighting, Patton sought a greater role for his Army, and decided to try to capture the capital, Palermo. After dispatching a 'reconnaissance' toward the town of Agrigento that succeeded in capturing it, he formed a provisional Corps and persuaded Alexander to allow him to continue to advance.

Alexander changed his mind and countermanded his orders, but Patton claimed the countermand was 'garbled in transmission' and by the time the position had been clarified Patton was at the gates of Palermo. Although there was little tactical value in taking the city, the rapid advance was an important demonstration of the US Army's mobility and skill, at a time when the reputation of US forces was still recovering from their losses at the ill-fated Battle of Kasserine Pass.

The fall of Palermo inspired a *coup d'état* against Mussolini, and he was deposed from power. Although the removal of Italy from the war had been one of the long-term objectives of the Italian

US Army tank in Sicily.

campaign, the suddenness of the move caught the Allies by surprise.

After Patton's capture of Palermo, with the British still bogged down south of Messina, Alexander ordered a two-pronged attack on the city. Montgomery suggested on July 24th to Patton that the Seventh U.S. Army take Messina, since they were in a better position to do so.

The invasion of Sicily achieved one of its goals, the downfall of Mussolini leaving Hitler alone of the Axis alliance.

The Axis Armies, now effectively under the command of German General Hans Hube, had prepared and controlled a strong defensive line, the 'Etna Line' around Messina that would enable them to make a progressive retreat while evacuating large parts of the Army to the mainland of Italy.

Patton began his assault on the line at Troina, but it was a linchpin of the defence and stubbornly held. Despite three 'end run' amphibious landings the Germans managed to keep the bulk of their forces beyond reach of capture, and maintain their evacuation plans. Elements of the U.S. 3rd Infantry Division entered Messina just hours after the last Axis troops boarded ship for Italy.

US Army forces enter Palermo.

However, Patton had won his race to enter Messina first. Operation Baytown was planned to land troops near the tip of Calabria (the "toe" of Italy) in connection with the invasion of Italy. Not to prevent an Axis escape from Sicily was a major strategic blunder. As a result, instead of a major Axis defeat and the fall of an enemy government, Operation Husky served as a prelude to a long and bloody campaign that probably prolonged World War II. Again, the Ultra information to hand had not been fully utilised.

The casualties on the Axis side totaled 29,000, with 140,000 (mostly Italians) captured. The US lost 2,237 killed and 6,544 wounded and captured; the British suffered 2,721 dead, and

British troops with a real trophy!

10,122 wounded and captured; the Canadians suffered 2,310 casualties including 562 killed in action. For many of the American forces, and the entire Canadian contingent, this was their first time in combat.

However, unfortunately the Axis successfully evacuated over 100,000 men and thousands of vehicles from Sicily that the Allies were unable to prevent. Rescuing such a large number of troops from the threat of capture represented a major success for the Axis. In the face of overwhelming Allied naval and air superiority, this evacuation was a major Allied failure, the more so since so much intelligence about the German/Italian forces existed courtesy of our Interception stations, Bletchley Park and the Ultra they provided out to our Generals – via SCU/SLUs.

Nevertheless, the invasion may have had an impact on the Russian front. One of the reasons Hitler gave for calling off his offensive near Kursk, was a decision to send units to Italy after receiving news of the invasion of Sicily.

Appendix 11

Mobile Construction and the SCU/SLUs

Section VIII was involved in many aspects of communication, including fitting aircraft with 'Ascension' the air-to-agent contact system devised in Whaddon workshops, on fitting its own designed wireless sets to MTBs, MGBs (Motor Gun Boats) for agent and intercept work and a whole host of very specialised tasks. Until early 1943, this work was carried out on an ad-hoc basis by several departments.

Dennis Smith, a brilliant wireless engineer, was a leading member of Section VIII's Research and Development (R&D) team designing new sets. He had been particularly involved with the design of the gear for Ascension. However, he was asked to form a separate department to bring this very diverse work together 'under-one-roof' so to speak. It was called 'Mobile Construction' and he was allocated a hut as his office and team workshop, just opposite the exit gate of Whaddon Hall.

He was free to choose his own team and I felt very fortunate to be included – even as its most junior member. The team was small, never more than nine, including Dennis Smith but he had chosen some very talented engineers. It developed into a varied and exciting life for me with flying in various aircraft,

Dennis Smith: Head of the Mobile Construction department of MI6 Section VIII and my boss from 1943 to 1945.

A Lockheed Hudson of the type used at Tempsford in Bedfordshire. We installed air-to-ground wireless gear called 'Ascension' to contact our agents on the ground in occupied territory. We also used Lockheed Venturas that are very similar in appearance.

working on MTBs and MGBs, and much more. We travelled widely to work on several different airfields, and to ports down in the West Country, such as Brixham, Teignmouth and Dartmouth.

In early 1944 our team at Mobile Construction was concentrating on installing wireless equipment into special vans, intended to pass 'Ultra' messages to our Military Commanders in the field during the battles to reoccupy Europe, after 'D-Day'.

These mobile SLU wireless stations were not a new idea in MI6 Section VIII. The first two had been created by Richard Gambier-Parry's team in 1940 and sent to supply Bletchley Park's early output to the BEF in France. The newly formed Mobile Construction made a few for use in North Africa in early 1943, including, I recall, two into Bedford QL4x4 that had been standard Army wireless control vehicles.

Dennis Smith in flying gear. Dennis was a member of the R and D team at Whaddon Hall who devised this invaluable system. He would sometimes go on operations but my flights – similarly attired but being under 19 – were limited to testing over the UK. However, we did drift over the Channel once or twice flying in North American B25 Mitchell's from Hartford Bridge.

A Royal Navy MGB (Motor Gun Boat) often based in Dartmouth and Brixham and fitted with our wireless gear. We also ran smaller MTBs (Motor Torpedo Boats). All these were used to carry agents and supplies across the Channel, as well as some interception.

Edgar's brother Wallace joined us in Mobile Construction in early 1944. He was occupied solely on the mobile SLU aspect of our many activities, and his workbench was alongside mine. It was from him that I first heard about Edgar.

Perhaps the pinnacle of the mobile SLU system was the wireless vans provided to our Military Commanders – on and after 'D-Day'. The vehicles used for the intended British and Canadian sectors, were ordinary army Guy 15 cwt wireless vans, stripped of their standard army wireless equipment and Whaddon design fittings installed instead. That included our famous MkIII transmitter and a National HRO receiver from the US. Mobile Construction carried out all the work.

In all, we created about eight for British/Canadian forces and about the same number in Dodge vehicles for the US forces. These wireless vans were intended to handle Ultra traffic directly from Bletchley Park (via the SCU wireless station at Windy Ridge in

This is a remarkable photograph. It shows three of the seven or eight Guy Wireless vans being fitted out at SCU/SLUs at Mobile Construction by the exit gate at Whaddon Hall. It is remarkable because of the great secrecy surrounding this work and shows the equipment being used. The men with braces showing are army wireless operators from SCU7 shown the wireless vans they are to take into Europe after 'D-Day'.

The Section VIII men in the picture are, Norman Stanton in the door of the left hand vehicle, Wallace Harrison (Edgar's brother standing near central with his head inclined to one side, and myself looking out of the right hand van.

These vans would have been attached to the HQ of such as General Montgomery, General Dempsey of 21st Army Group, and General Crerar commanding the Canadian forces at 'D-Day'.

Whaddon village) right into the headquarters of the Allied Military Commanders – at the highest level.

On the British and Canadian sectors, these would have included General Montgomery, General Dempsey Commanding the 21st Army Group, General Crerar of the Canadian forces and others for the Air Force Commanders in the field. Another, for example, was attached to the 2nd SAS as part of the SAS Brigade. That in turn, became part of Lieut. General 'Boy' Browning's British First Airborne Corps.

In the American sector, we utilised brand new US Army Dodge ambulances. The stretchers were removed and identical wireless gear was fitted as we used in the Guy 15cwt vans for the British sectors. The converted Dodge ambulances were destined for United States Generals commanding the Army and Army Air Corps of the US forces about to embark for Europe. One of our Dodge 'ambulances' went to General Patton's 3rd Army, another to General Bradley, to General Simpson, to General Pete Quesada commanding the US 9th Army Air Force – and so on.

Someone of great authority must have taken the picture shown since these vehicles were the live end of the Ultra system – Britain's greatest wartime secret. It shows three of the Guy vans with their equipment, on two benches, taken out for the photograph. On each bench you will see the wireless gear, left to right an HRO, a Marconi Morse key and then the Mk III transmitter.

Wallace Harrison (Edgar's brother) is standing fifth from the right. I am the young engineer leaning out of the window of the right hand Guy SLU.

When Edgar returned home at the end of 1943 he carried out a variety of tasks including training more operators to supply SCU8 in France. However, curiously he later took charge of an SCU/SLU team based around one of these wireless equipped Dodge ambulances that Wallace had help build. He took Wallace with him as one of his operator/engineers into France and on to Germany.

Around the same time as we converted the Guy vans for the British and Canadian sectors, we fitted the same wireless and associated gear into Dodge Ambulances for such as General's Patton, Bradley, 'Pete' Quesada and Simpson. The picture taken at Bletchley Park in 2003, shows a Dodge Ambulance just as we received them with me standing in front.

Appendix 12

Winston Churchill's Conferences where Edgar Harrison was in attendance as his Ultra wireless operator.

F. W. Winterbotham describes in his book 'The Ultra Secret' how he was asked to furnish a secure Ultra connection for Churchill during his travels abroad. Apparently he received a polite message from Downing Street *'Pray make the necessary arrangements'*. Thus Churchill always had a secure channel for Ultra, and for his own messages, provided by Gambier-Parry's Section VIII. Using only a low powered agent's set would mean that his wireless messages, originating in the Middle East for example, would have been relayed on from our station at Cairo, through to 'Main Line' at Whaddon and thence to London.

During the 1943 conference in Cairo, Winston Churchill took time off to visit troops in the desert. He was always pleased to meet and talk to servicemen in battle zones.

The 1943 conference in Cairo between Churchill, Roosevelt and General Chiang Kai-Shek.

Ultra from Bletchley Park and Mr. Churchill's own Top Secret messages from London would have used the same route in reverse i.e. 'Main Line' at Whaddon Hall, Cairo and on to the Section VIII wireless operator accompanying his party.

Edgar Harrison was chosen to provide that service in the Middle East theatre and travelled as Churchill's Section VIII – SCU operator on several of his journeys in the area. He listed conferences in Cairo, Mersin, Nicosia, Teheran and Yalta but offered no details of them in his files or papers except that it is plain, he regarded Mersin and the follow up meetings at Nicosia, as two of them. As Edgar was stationed in or around Cairo so often, it is not surprising to find it on the list. There may well have been a number of meetings on different visits in the Cairo area that Edgar mentions just once.

The Teheran conference that followed the meeting in Cairo between Mr. Churchill, Mr. Roosevelt and Stalin.

He gave details of only one Conference – that at Mersin – and an anecdote connected with another. He would have used one of the Whaddon made agents' suitcase sets (almost certainly a MkVII) to provide a wireless service for the Great Man. An immediate problem now is the places and the time frame. Anything I write would be only guesswork, as he passed away before I had reached near this point with him. Perhaps I should resist any guesswork in view of Churchill's comment to Edgar *'You either know Harrison or you don't know!'*

The Yalta conference between Mr. Churchill, Mr. Roosevelt and Stalin.

The Churchill Archives at Churchill College Cambridge, have kindly given me a list of visits made abroad by Mr. Churchill. I think however, in view of the importance of Edgar's role in handling ULTRA signals and Churchill's top level messages at these historic meetings, it would be wrong to go beyond what we *do* know!

Appendix 13

Agents' wireless sets made at Whaddon Hall

On his travels with Winston Churchill, Edgar refers to carrying an 'Agent's small transceiver' and that can only mean the MkVII since our earlier MkV was bulky and heavy. Indeed, the MkV was being phased out of production when I joined in 1942. Nevertheless, my very first job was deburring the rough edges of the cut steel plates, that formed the MkV chassis – perhaps they were among the last batches of MkVs made? However, I was aware that the smaller MkVII set was already in limited production in the metal workshop where I had started my training.

Indeed, more MkVII sets were eventually made than any other Whaddon design. Numbers built exceeded even the famous MkIII transmitter that had become standard throughout SCU's work, at home and abroad as well as with agents. I should add that the metal workshop did much more than make just the chassis for the sets. It made complete Morse keys – in the case of the MkVII – these were built-in through the chassis itself – so as to be almost flush. It designed and created the front of sets, like the MkIII, in plastic, and indeed carried out a raft of work from design

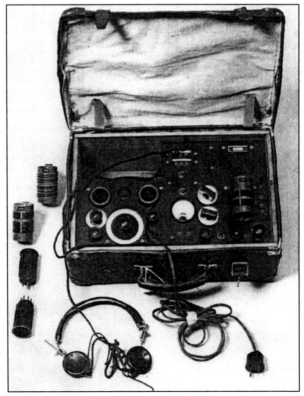

The MkV transceiver wireless set designed and manufactrured by the R&D team at Whaddon Hall. It was bulky and heavy for an agent to carry and later replaeed by the MkVII.

through to production. The chassis, fronts and components were then passed into the wireless assembly rooms, where they were wired and assembled, thus becoming wireless sets for different purposes.

Production of the MkVII was started in early 1942, and the set was clearly going to be a great success, requiring more production space than could be provided in the huts in the grounds of Whaddon Hall. An extensive farm-garage workshop was found a few miles away, within SCU7's Little Horwood camp. It was immediately put out of bounds to the troops housed nearby who were employed as the unit's despatch riders, drivers, motor mechanics, cooks, guards and so on.

The MkIII was probably the most successful set to come out of Whaddon. It was used in fixed SLUs, in our mobile units and in Embassy wireless rooms when MI6 operators were employed.

The garage was fitted out with heating, machinery, work benches, stores and offices towards the end of 1942, and in January 1943 the first transfers from Whaddon took place (including myself), into the new metal workshop – originally devoted to making the MkVII – along with some MkIIIs. Hughie Castleman was put in overall charge with Bert Norman in charge of the metal workshops where I was to work.

The MkVII was first of all conceived as a suitcase set for agents and hundreds were made for that purpose. However, it also became the stand-by set for SCU/SLU mobile units, in the event of technical problems with their standard equipment of MkIII transmitter and American built receiver, the National HRO.

The MkVII metal chassis was set into a wood casing made there by Len Warner. The 'suitcase set' meant exactly that and hundreds of small leather cases were supplied from my father's wireless store based in the

This is an early version of the MkVII transceiver – a true suitcase set – and one that was put into large production in the new Little Horwood 'factory'. It was followed by the 'Cash box' or 'Paraset' version in a metal case known as the MkVII/2.

Stables at Whaddon Hall. I think we can be fairly sure that the *agent's small transceiver* described by Edgar and used on his journeys with Mr. Churchill was a MkVII – in a leather case.

However, the set was later put into large production as the 'cashbox' version with a hinged metal lid, later to become known as the 'Paraset'.

(Several versions of the MkVII can be seen in the Wireless Museum at Bletchley Park including one in a small leather case – similar to one used by Edgar Harrison).

Appendix 14

Countries in which Edgar served or visited between 1933 and 1975

Below you will find a list of countries visited by Edgar during his lifetime of service in the army, in MI6 (Section VIII) and in the Diplomatic Wireless Service (DWS) the communication division of the Foreign and Commonwealth Office.

To understand the sheer number of countries involved it is important to appreciate not only the breadth of his Army service but also the importance of the diplomatic career that followed it.

You will have seen how he started training as a boy-apprentice in the Royal Corps of Signals in 1929 and how that eventually led him to a long term of service in China. He mentions visiting many of the Chinese provinces and his wartime career led him to serve in many parts of Europe and the Middle East. After the war he became a member of the Diplomatic Wireless Service (DWS) and ended his career as its Principal Signals Officer with responsibility for its communications across the world.

In the Royal Corps of Signals

Far East 1933-1938
China, Inner Mongolia, Outer Mongolia, Siberia, Manchuria, Korea, Sinkiang, Tibet, Hong Kong.

In MI6 (Section VIII)

Middle East and Europe 1939-1945
Norway, France, Belgium, Gibraltar, Malta, Egypt, Greece, Albania, Crete, Cyprus, Turkey, Yugoslavia, Palestine, Syria, Iraq, Armenia, Georgia, Ukraine, Iran, Jordan, Sudan, Cyrenaica, Tripolitania, Tunisia, Algeria, Sicily, Italy, Holland, Germany, Crimea.

In the Diplomatic Wireless Service

Far East 1945-1949
Japan, Hong Kong, Formosa.

Indian sub-continent 1949-1952
India, Pakistan, Ceylon, Afghanistan, Nepal, Bhutan, Sikkim, Burma.

Far East 1953-1955
Singapore, Malaya.

Europe 1956-1958
Denmark, Sweden, Finland, Russia

Middle East and Africa 1958-1961
Lebanon, Jordan, Kuwait, North Yemen, South Yemen, Bahrain, Arab Emirates, Iraq, Iran, Turkey, Egypt, Libya, Tunisia, Algeria, Saudi Arabia, Eritrea, Ethiopia, Sudan, Kenya, Somaliland, Chad, Uganda, Zanzibar, Tanzania, Greece, Italy.

Indian sub-continent 1961-1963
As for 1949-1952 plus Tibet, Bangladesh.

Far East 1964-1967
Singapore, Malaya, Thailand, Cambodia, Laos, Vietnam, Borneo, Philippines, Indonesia, Burma, Hong Kong, Taiwan, Korea, Japan, China, New Guinea, New Zealand.

World wide 1967-1975 as the Principal Signals Officer of the Diplomatic Wireless Service
Zambia, Botswana, Zimbabwe, Mozambique, Malawi, Zaire, South Africa, St. Helena, Tristan da Cunha, Angola, Ghana, Gambia, Hawaii, Nigeria, USA, Australia, Fiji.

Driving licences held

China, Hong Kong, Egypt, Russia, Greece, Japan, India, Pakistan, Singapore, Malaya, Sudan, Palestine, and Australia.

Appendix 15

The Sections of SIS (MI6)
forming the organisation in 1939

Chief of the SIS (CSS) Admiral Sir Hugh Sinclair, known as 'C'.

I. Political Section.

II. Military Section under Colonel Stewart Menzies. He was to become 'C' on the death of Admiral Sir Hugh Sinclair in November 1939.

III. Naval Section.

IV. Air Section under Wing Commander Fred Winterbotham, RAF.

V. Counter Espionage Section.

VI. Industrial Section.

VII. Finance Section under Commander Percy Sykes R.N.

VIII. Communications Section, under Colonel Richard Gambier-Parry.

IX. Cipher Section.

X. Press Section.

Note: There is some ambiguity about the numbering of two of the Sections. It concerns II (Military) and IV (Air). Some authorities insist that II was Air and IV was Military and even that the two changed numbers at some point!

I have chosen to use the identical lists as shown, firstly in Anthony Cave-Brown's monumental work on Stewart Menzies *"The Secret Servant – The life of Sir Stewart Menzies – Churchill's Spymaster."* Secondly, Nigel West's *"MI6 – British Secret Intelligence Service Operations 1909-45."*

Before finalising the drafts of this book, and in an attempt to be absolutely sure on the point, I have twice contacted SIS HQ at Vauxhall Cross in London about it. They have, incidentally, recently become more helpful since the days when I was writing 'The Secret Wireless War' but strangely, they will not confirm which is correct. Seeing they are being asked about just a detail from around 70 years ago, I find their silence on the point curious.

However, the number of the more important Section – so far as this book is concerned – is seemingly not in dispute. Edgar (and others like myself) was definitely in Section VIII, under its Head, Richard Gambier-Parry.

Bibliography

A number of authors have been of great assistance to me in preparing this book about Edgar Harrison. Below, I refer to several who have had a direct bearing on my work and a number who provided background material for 'The Secret Wireless War' that has also been useful in this project. I thank them all.

Books dealing specifically with the areas where Edgar operated.

'Crete. The battle and the Resistance.'

This is by Antony Beevor the author of a number of acclaimed books on World War II, including: 'Paris after the Liberation' – 'Stalingrad' – ' Berlin: The downfall 1945' and 'Crete. The Battle and the Resistance'. It was the latter book that I found particularly helpful.

I knew Edgar Harrison, 'Curly' Meadows and 'Dinger' Bell were handling the Ultra traffic on Crete but Antony's book supplied a great deal of information about the German attack and the defence led by General Freyberg V.C. the Officer Commanding the Allied troops. I am truly grateful to him for permission to quote from this excellent book.

'Ultra and Mediterranean Strategy.'

By Ralph Bennett. This is a brilliantly researched book by a man who was working at Bletchley Park on decrypts himself in World War II and then records many more of them following his later research at the Public Records Office at Kew. It is a broad ranging book covering the battles and the use of Ultra throughout the Mediterranean.

'The Forgotten 500.'

By Gregory A. Freeman. This excellent book claims to be 'The untold story of the men who risked all for the greatest rescue mission of World War II.' Whether this claim is right or wrong is not relevant here. It deals in great detail with the way the Chetnik forces in Yugoslavia rescued so many US Airmen and the long delay in presenting General Mihailovic with his Legion of Merit awarded to him by President Harry S. Truman in 1948.

Tito had Mihailovic executed in July 1946. However, due to the 'political change' with the West then supporting Tito, it was decided not to present the award. It was only in 2005, that his Legion of Merit – awarded in 1948 was presented to his family – long after Tito's death.

Books with general information on Ultra and the wider SIS scene.

These cover the work at Bletchley Park, the 'Y' service and other operations that had connections with MI6 (Section VIII).

'A History of The British Secret Service.'
By Richard Deacon, published by Frederick Muller Ltd.

'MI6' and 'GCHQ'.
Both are by Nigel West and published by Weidenfeld & Nicolson. They are full of detail and are a necessary read for those wishing to know more about the general history of both organisations.

'Spycatcher'
By Peter Wright, was first published by Viking Penguin in 1987. Whilst this is largely about his own career in MI5, the early chapters refer to his father's close connection with the Marconi organisation and SIS in World War I. It indicates a probable link between the Marconi wireless factory in Barnes High Street in West London, and the placing of the SIS wireless station in the huge Metropolitan Police complex, a few hundred metres away. Subsequently, in 1938, the station moved only a short distance along the Thames riverside to 'Florence House'. This empty printing works was purchased in 1938 by Richard Gambier-Parry to become the new SIS Wireless Station.

'The Secret Servant - the life of Sir Stewart Menzies - Churchill's spymaster'.
By Anthony Cave Brown published by Sphere Books Limited. This is a real insight into the life of this man who became 'C' – Chief of SIS – in 1939. It is most likely that it was Menzies who suggested to Admiral Sir Hugh Sinclair that his friend Richard Gambier-Parry become the Head of the Wireless Communications division of SIS – later to become MI6 (Section VIII).

'Ultra goes to War.'
An excellent and very detailed book by Ronald Lewin, detailing the work of Bletchley Park and its Ultra output. A must for students.

'Britain's best kept Secret - Ultra's base at Bletchley Park.'
This publication is by Ted Enever who was a Founder Member of the Bletchley Park Trust. It is on sale at the Bletchley Park bookshop. A very comprehensive book covering the history of Bletchley Park itself, the arrival of SIS, a description of the work done during the war, the Huts, the Bombes, and Colossus.

He also importantly records that the MI6 wireless station – the so-called 'Station X' – was in the water tower of Bletchley Park Mansion but moved out to the nearby village of Whaddon as MI6 (Section VIII) acquired Whaddon Hall as its HQ in 1939.

'The Code breakers - The inside story of Bletchley Park.'
By F. H. Hinsley and Alan Striff. Quite technical in parts but a rewarding book to read; containing stories of the successes, and failures of the code breakers.

'England Needs You - the story of Beaumanor.'
By Joan Nicholls who was in the ATS as an operator in the 'Y' (Wireless Interception) unit at Beaumanor. Her book is available from the Bletchley Park bookshop. This is an important book for those wishing to learn about the Y service and its importance as part of the Ultra Trilogy.

'The Ultra Secret' by F. W. Winterbotham.
I was grateful to Weidenfeld and Nicolson for permission to quote from this book in 'The Secret Wireless War'. It was written by Group-Captain Fred Winterbotham who had been head of MI6 Section IV (Air) during the War. He seemed to break ranks with senior SIS officers in writing the book back in 1974, when Bletchley Park and the word 'Ultra' were still unknown to the public. Furthermore, we were still being advised not to discuss our wartime work.

He constantly refers to 'Special Liaison Units', in fact they appear in his index over thirty times. Yet, although he takes a proprietary approach to the whole SLU network, not once does he mention that the wireless units were designed, built and run by MI6 (Section VIII). Furthermore, there is no mention of Brigadier Gambier-Parry, of Whaddon, of Section VIII, or even of SCUs.

Writing about the Special Liaison Unit staff at the headquarters of the 9th US Tactical Air Force, he says *'I had put an American officer in charge of the SLU unit here, with the usual complement of RAF cypher sergeants and W/T personnel.'* He omits to say that the *'W/T personnel'*, and all their equipment, were provided entirely by Gambier-Parry's SCU organisation.

One of the wireless operators was a colleague, Bernard Gildersleve of SCU8. (See Chapter 36 of my book 'The Secret Wireless War'). Bernard was attached to the 9th US TAC under its Commanding Officer – Major General Elwood 'Pete' Quesada. He was in a Dodge wireless vehicle SCU/SLU converted from a US Army ambulance by the Mobile Construction team under Dennis Smith, including myself, at Whaddon Hall. For a number of reasons therefore, I join others critical of Winterhbotham, his timing, and inaccuracy.

'British Intelligence in the Second World War' (Vol. IV). By F.H. Hinsley, and C.A.G. Simkins. HMSO, 1990.

The Secret Wireless War. I published 'The Secret Wireless War' in 2003, after some seven years of research. There was very little for me to go on, seeing the subject of the MI6 (Section VIII) Wireless Communications of World War II was still treated by the authorities with total secrecy. I was fortunate that some of my old colleagues were able to help towards the work. I believe it is a true record of the unit's great contribution to the war effort. It is already a known source of information for others whilst being useful to me in production of this book for Edgar Harrison.

Index